FLEET STREET

THE STORY OF A STREET

FLEET STREET

THE STORY OF A STREET

ALAN BROOKE

AMBERLEY

First published 2010

Amberley Publishing
Cirencester Road, Chalford,
Stroud, Gloucestershire, GL6 8PE

www.amberley-books.com

British Library Cataloguing in Publication Data.
A catalogue record for this book is available from the British Library.

ISBN 978 1 84868 229 0

Typesetting and origination by Amberley Publishing
Printed in Great Britain

CONTENTS

INTRODUCTION

Fleet Street is one of the most ancient and celebrated thoroughfares in London. Its name was long synonymous with the press but this masks an equally rich history. Although the street was outside the old City Wall, its proximity made it important both as a highway and residential district. For centuries it has been famous for its association with newspapers, printers, stationers, booksellers, taverns, coffee houses, banking houses, the legal profession, places of worship, exhibitions, and processions. Additionally, many famous people have lived in or frequented the street as well as the multitude of alleys, lanes, streets, and courts that lead from it.

When the London historian Edwin Beresford Chancellor (1868-1937) wrote *The Annals of Fleet Street: Its Traditions and Associations* in 1912 he commented that there has never before been a history of Fleet Street written (*Fleet Street in Seven Centuries* by W. G. Bell was also published in 1912).

Since Chancellor's observation nearly 100 years ago, books specifically on the history of the street have continued to be thin on the ground. What books have been produced have varied from those dealing with the history of the press, compilations of old photographs of the street, and some that include Fleet Street along with St Paul's and Holborn or focus on a particular part of the street such as St. Bride's Church or the Inns of Court.

Fleet Street, with other famous names such as Oxford Street and Regent Street, would be one of at least half a dozen London streets that most people would be able to name. Yet despite its fame and its history, Fleet Street is only a relatively short stretch of road. The east end of the street, near Ludgate Circus, is where the River Fleet ran against the medieval walls of the City whilst at the west end is Temple Bar, which marks the present City limits. Fleet Street then merges into the Strand near the Royal Courts of Justice. To the south of Fleet Street is the Temple, a complex of buildings that were once the property of the Knights Templar.

The history of Fleet Street is diverse, fascinating, turbulent and full of colourful characters and events. London's second most important river ran through it and gave the street its name. Carmelite Friars occupied the area between today's Whitefriars Street and the Temple. From the fourteenth century the military order of the Knights Templar were replaced by the legal profession who permanently settled in the area. Part of the street was ravaged by the Great Fire and then again by Second World War bombs. The street was a showplace for freaks, fire-eaters, giants, dwarfs, elephants and other exotic exhibits. The Automobile Association opened its first offices in 1905 at No. 18. Many notable people have lived, worked, and drank in Fleet Street, especially in famous watering holes such as the *Cheshire Cheese* and *El Vino's*. The press had an early presence in the street. William Caxton's assistant, Wynkyn de Worde, was the first printer to set up shop in Fleet Street in the late fifteenth century and Britain's first newspaper, the *Daily Courant,* began to publish there in 1702. Fleet Street once boasted the headquarters of virtually every major English daily newspaper until most relocated from the 1980s to Wapping, the Isle of Dogs and Docklands. In 2005 the news agency Reuters was among the last remaining press organisations when it vacated its premises on Fleet Street after sixty-six years. As the newspapers left so did much of the atmosphere of what journalist Christopher Hitchens called that 'little enclave between Ludgate Circus and the Strand.'

CHAPTER ONE

THE RIVER FLEET

The River Fleet, commonly known as the Fleet Ditch, was London's second great river until it became so polluted it was covered over from the eighteenth century. As well as giving its name to Fleet Street, the river also shaped much of the early history of the street. The discovery of artefacts found there show evidence of earlier settlements. During the 1670s, when the river was widened, various Roman, British, and Saxon antiquities of interest were discovered. The finds included coins, arrowheads, broad spur rowels, keys, daggers, scales, ships' counters with Saxon characters, and medals, crosses, and crucifixes, of a later date. Urns containing the bones of Romans were unearthed in Shoe Lane, the first known Roman cemetery, west of the River Fleet. In the early 1990s archaeological excavation found evidence of industrial activity dating from the early Roman period on the east side of the Fleet estuary, and it has been suggested that a tide-mill existed there.

Between AD 50 and AD 410 Londinium was the largest city in Britannia and was pre-eminent as a port, where goods were imported from all over the known world. When the City wall was constructed around AD 200 it enclosed substantial areas of unoccupied land, and encompassed the military fort at Cripplegate and the west bank of the River Fleet.

The River Fleet starts from a number of springs north of central London on Hampstead Heath. There are two main sources, one on either side of Parliament Hill, both about 350 feet above sea level. The streams are dammed into the Highgate and Hampstead Ponds. From Hampstead the two streams run downhill, mostly underground in culverts and pipes, through Kentish Town and Camden, joining together south of Camden Town. The name of the river is traced, by some, to the Anglo-Saxon *fleotan* – 'to float' and by others to the Saxon *fleot* – tidal inlet. By the Anglo-Saxon period the Fleet was still a substantial body of water and was used as a dock for shipping. The Fleet was fed by many springs and numerous wells that were built along its banks such as Clerkenwell, Bagnigge Well, Skinner's Well, Fogg's Well, Tod's Well, Rad Well and St. Bride's Well, which were all believed to have healing qualities. The Fleet was called 'the River of Wells' as early as the days of William the Conqueror.

In medieval times, the Fleet was navigable as far as Holborn and provided a useful trade route into the City. There is no indication of when the first bridge across the River was built although it was probably during the Roman occupation. John Stow (1525-1605) wrote in his *Survey of London* (1598) that there was 'a bridge of stone, fair coped

Entrance to the Fleet River, Samuel Scott, c. 1750

on either side with iron pikes'. This bridge fell victim to the Great Fire of 1666 and was replaced by a much wider one bearing the arms of the City. Stow in fact described five bridges over the lower part of the Fleet and added that before 1307 ten or twelve ships used to go up the Fleet to Fleet Bridge 'with divers things and merchandises, and some of these ships went under the bridge unto Holborn Bridge'. The course of the Fleet from Holborn to the Thames can be seen on maps such as those of Ralph Aggas 1563, Wenceslaus Hollar 1666, and John Rocque's Map of London, 1746.

From a very early period the Fleet was used for many purposes, from the turning of watermills to the reception of refuse and offal of every description. Tanneries and slaughterhouses lined the banks of the Fleet where the dyes and blood turned the river various shades of red. In 1307 the Calendar of Patent Rolls recorded that 'the water course of the Fleet is said to be obstructed and straitened by mud and filth being thrown into it'. By 1357 anyone throwing rubbish into the river was threatened with imprisonment.

The Fleet, which resembled an inland port, dominated the medieval suburb with varied river craft moored alongside the bank. Long before Fleet Street became famous for printing, its main industry was leather, and reeking tanneries lined the river, preparing hides for boots, shoes, saddlery, and other leather items. Off Farringdon Street is Seacoal Lane, whose name can be traced back to 1228 when a wharf at its base was used by barges taking seaborne coal on the River Fleet. However, it is also suggested that Seacoal Lane was so named because it was a residential area where coal merchants once lived. Whatever the reason, the name reflects the very early beginning of the importation of coal into London. The lane also marks the boundaries of the old Fleet Prison.

As the area around Fleet Street expanded and became busier, the problem of noxious exhalations emanating from the Fleet proved too much for local residents. In 1290, the Prior of the Carmelite house that stood in the area west of the present Whitefriars Street complained of the stench and miasma that had killed many of the hooded brethren. The awful stink was so great that it even overpowered the smell of the incense. Other residents, including the Bishop of Salisbury whose palace was in Salisbury Court to the south east of Fleet Street, made similar complaints. However, Walter Thornbury commented in *Old and New London vol. 2* (1878), that in 'the year 1502 . . . the intolerable Fleet Ditch was cleared, from Holborn to the Thames, and it became once more navigable for large barges, laden with fuel and fish'. It did not last and in 1652 the sewer was thoroughly cleansed, but the ditch had now become impassable to boats because of the numerous pigsties on the banks and the vast quantities of offal and garbage thrown in by the butchers.

Clearly such good intentions to keep the river navigable and clean were futile. Ben Jonson (*Famous Voyage, c.1612*) told a tale of two Londoners who hired an open boat to row up the sewage-clogged Fleet Ditch that he described as follows: 'Your Fleet-Lane Furies; and hot cooks do dwell, That with still-scalding steams, make the place hell.' By the end of the century the satirist Jonathan Swift gave a vivid picture of how the Fleet was just a depository for all types of filth: 'Seapings from butcher's stalls, dung, guts and blood, drowned puppies, stinking sprats, all drenched in mud, dead cats and turnip-tops come tumbling down into the flood.' Alexander Pope (*Dunciad*, 1728) commenting on the Fleet: 'the king of dykes! Rolls the large tribute of dead dogs to Thames'.

The ditch also suffered from occasional floods before it was covered. In 1679, after heavy rains, it broke down at the back of several wholesale butchers and carried off cattle, dead and alive. It was not uncommon for shops and houses around Fleet Street and Farringdon Road to experience regular flood damage. An outbreak of cholera in Clerkenwell Prison in 1832 was attributed to the effluvia of the River Fleet. Even after it was closed the outflow into the Thames was fraught with problems. John Wykeham Archer, in his *Vestiges of Old London* (1851) noted that at the opening to the Thames

> Many persons enter at low tide, armed with sticks to defend themselves from rats, as well as for the purpose of sounding on their perilous way among the slimy shallows; and carrying a lantern to light the dreary passage . . . Many venturers have been struck down in such a dismal pilgrimage, to be heard of no more; many have fallen suddenly choked, sunk bodily in the treacherous slime, become a prey to swarms of voracious rats, or have been overwhelmed by a sudden increase of the polluted stream.

However, during the eighteenth century the Fleet's long history as an open river was coming to an end. In 1733, the City of London petitioned the House of Commons for permission to cover the ditch, as all navigation had by then ceased. In addition, the Fleet had become impossible to clean, and several people had fallen in and been suffocated in the mud. In 1763, a drunken barber, from Bromley in Kent, was found in Fleet Ditch, standing upright and frozen to death. By 1766 the old landmark was to be no more and it was covered over between Fleet Street and the Thames.

Over the following years the rest of the river was covered piece by piece.

The outflow of the Fleet at Blackfriars

The busy stretch that was covered to make way for Farringdon Street between Holborn and Ludgate Circus formed the Fleet Market. This was opened on 30 September 1737 for the sale of meat, fish, and vegetables. In 1829 the thoroughfare from Holborn to Blackfriars Bridge was widened and Fleet Market was removed. On the east side of the market, between Ludgate Hill and Fleet Lane, was the Fleet Prison. However, an unofficial market existed in this area before 1737. In his *London Spy* (1703) Ned Ward moralized about the 'vices and vanities of the Town'. In his meanderings around Fleet Bridge (that linked Fleet Street and Ludgate Street) he observed that

> nuts, gingerbread, oranges and oysters, lay piled up in moveable shops that run upon wheels, attended by ill-looking fellows, some with but one eye, and others without noses. Over against these stood a parcel of trugmoldies [old prostitutes] in straw hats or flat-caps, selling socks and furmity [a dish made mainly from boiled, cracked wheat and milk, eggs or broth] nightcaps and plum pudding.

By the 1870s the upper reaches of the River Fleet disappeared in culverts beneath the new suburbs of Hampstead and Kentish Town.

The River Fleet today now serves as an underground storm relief sewer, continuing its course from Hampstead where it initially flows in two paths before joining up and passing under Belsize Park, Kentish Town and King's Cross and then continuing onto Clerkenwell, Farringdon Street, under Holborn Viaduct, Ludgate Circus, and joining the Thames near Blackfrairs Bridge. Its valley can be detected in various places (for example, between Clerkenwell and Holborn). It is also said that it in quieter moments it can be heard flowing through the grating in front of the *Coach and Horses* pub in Ray Street, Farringdon. After its journey of over 4 miles, the Fleet finally flows (more often trickles) into the Thames at Blackfriars through an underground system of brickwork tunnels ranging mostly from eight feet to twenty feet high.

CHAPTER TWO

EARLY HISTORY
OF FLEET STREET

At the time of the Roman settlement Fleet Street was little more than a rough road running through open country. The oldest part of the street is that closest to the pre-Roman settlement around Ludgate. Remaining parts of Saxon London after the Norman Conquest were largely destroyed in the fire that took much of the City in 1135. According to the *Liber Albus* ('White Book' compiled in 1419 that documents much of London's medieval history) the fire burnt from London Bridge to St. Clement Danes.

We have established that Fleet Street took its name from the River Fleet but it was generally known as Fleet Bridge Street at an earlier date, on account of the bridge that carried the roadway over the stream. This earlier name of Fleet Bridge (or Fletebrigge) is mentioned in 1228 in the *Liber Albus* in association with Henry de Buke who killed one Le Ireis le Tylor here, and fled to Southwark for sanctuary. Another reference is made in the Calendar of Patent Rolls of 17 October 1265, which talks of a 'grant to John de Verdun, of those houses in the street of Flete late the property of John de Flete.' This is an interesting point as it indicates that the name had been used as a family designation. Its present name, Fleet Street, does not appear until around 1311.

Also around this time, the Black Friars or Dominicans came from Oxford and took up residence on the east side of Shoe Lane (or Shoe Alley as it was sometimes referred) between 1224 and 1278. They then moved to the south east of Fleet Street near to the River Thames, establishing a massive monastic complex. Their hugely impressive priory, which was dissolved in the Reformation of the 1530s, was rated among the largest religious houses in London.

Another religious order that played a significant part in the history of the area was the Carmelites or White Friars. The Carmelites originated from Mount Carmel, a coastal mountain range in north Israel. Under the patronage of Richard, Earl of Cornwall, the brother of King Henry II, some members of the order sailed to England and by 1253 had built a small church on Fleet Street. It was replaced by a much larger church a century later.

Their priory was located in the notorious area of Alsatia, a district that became known for its brothels and the rookery of criminals. The Calendar of Close Rolls of 1346 commented that the surrounding area of the Carmelite priory produced so much noise that the friars were often hindered in celebrating divine service. The records noted that 'all women of ill-fame dwelling in the west lane or in houses adjoining the place of the prior and brethren of the Carmelites are to be removed from those places, without delay'.

As the wealth of the Carmelites grew, their land expanded until it comprised all the area between Temple Bar at the western part of Fleet Street south to the Thames and east to what is now Whitefriars Street. Their land included gardens, orchards, various buildings, a library, extensive dormitories, a cemetery, and a magnificent church. However, by 1545 the Carmelite church was totally destroyed as a result of the Reformation, and the other buildings, kitchen, library, and the convent garden were granted to Richard Morrison, Henry VIII's armourer.

As London's population grew beyond the City Wall, houses and shops began to spring up along the once rural road of Fleet Street. In the Patent Rolls of 20 July 1321, Hugh de Strubbi bequeathed to his wife Sarra a tavern with eight shops in the parish of St. Bride. Also in 1321, a shop in Fleet Street supplied King Edward II with 'six pair of boots with tassels of silk and drops of silver gilt.' A measure of how Fleet Street was expanding is the fact that in 1325 it was referred to as being in the suburb of London.

Despite an urban expansion during this century, there were still open fields on the north side of Fleet Street, which lay behind a broken line of houses. In 1315, the people of Westminster petitioned King Edward II about the state of the road between Temple Bar and Westminster. It was so bad that the feet of horses and pedestrians were continually being injured and thickets and bushes interrupted the route. It seemed that over two hundred years later the situation remained pretty much the same. Although statutes were passed in 1540 and 1543 ordering Fleet Street and some of its tributaries to be paved with stone, the west part of Fleet Street was described in 1543 as foul and full of pits and sloughs, and very perilous and noisome. In addition there was so much concern regarding the accumulation of filth that there was an order demanding that the street be kept clean to avoid outbreaks of pestilence.

As for the buildings, there were a number of substantial houses in and around Fleet Street. However, the majority of houses were described as mean, suggesting that they had only one room. The shop-fronts were entirely open to the elements of the weather. Any adverse storm caused havoc, as in 1316 when Fleet Bridge was severely damaged and houses were destroyed and men, women and children were swept away in the flood. A common practice was that of cutting rushes from the banks of the Thames to line the floors of houses. In 1416 rushes were in such abundance that it was decreed that the boats carrying the rushes up the Fleet shall be 'taken into the hands of the Chamberlain . . . [who] shall cause all the streets to be cleansed.' Stone houses were not the norm and fire always presented the greatest threat to dwellings with timber-framed buildings.

London generally and Fleet Street particularly, were so heavily populated and overcrowded that in 1580 a royal proclamation prohibited any further building. Apart from the difficulties of governing so large a number of people, there were also the fears of ever-recurring plague and providing large numbers of inhabitants with the means of sustenance. The Agas map of 1563 shows that the south of Fleet Street was covered with buildings, including notable ones such as the royal palace of Bridewell. To the north of Fleet Street the houses were mainly confined to those lining the roadway. By the end of the sixteenth century the monastic orders and most of their buildings had been cleared from the area thus paving the way for slum rookeries. The problem of overcrowding was made worse by the increasing population of the City, which was spilling out into the suburb of Fleet Street. In the 1590s John Stow wrote of the 'fading grandeur' of the larger, old houses that were giving way to a maze of new, and often filthy, alleys and unpaved courts.

A proclamation of 1580 seems to have had little effect on this expansion, as Faithorne's map of 1658 shows both the north and south side of Fleet Street heavily populated with buildings of all sizes. The growing population of people and buildings was reflected in the bustle of street life. Parish records in the late sixteenth century refer to Fleet Street as 'the highstrete' or 'the highway'. The street would have been cobbled with no footpaths (these only really developed from 1614). Shopkeepers would shout to attract trade. Adam Lorrison was fined in 1619 for intruding his fruit stalls into the highway, much to the annoyance of passers-by, and Adam Harris found himself in trouble for 'exposing his baskets' in Fleet Street. Complaints were made against women in 1623 for selling fruit in the open street and for setting their stalls too far into the road.

Before the Great Fire of 1666 the houses along Fleet Street were made mainly of timber, and overhanging in all imaginable positions. The street was characterized by trade signs, these included images of animals, birds, fish, the sun and stars, often in glaring eye-catching colours. The *Spectator* commented that 'our streets are filled with Blue Boars, Black Swans and Red Lions, not to mention Flying Pigs, and Hogs in Armour, and many other creatures more extraordinary than any in the deserts of Africa'. The *Castle Tavern* in Fleet Street possessed the largest sign in London, 'almost obscuring the sun', whilst the barber's poles were described by a contemporary writer as looking 'as long as a mizzen mast'. These signs could pose a danger when they swung in the wind. The weight of the iron from which they were suspended brought street frontages down on a number of occasions, such as the time when the collapse of particular one building killed 'two young ladies, a cobbler and the King's jeweller'.

An important facility and landmark in the centre of Fleet Street was the conduit near Shoe Lane. In addition to supplying water for the area, it also played a role in civic proclamations and pageants such as that in 1533 when Anne Boleyn went to be crowned at Westminster. Instead of water, the conduit poured forth wine and was decorated with angels. Construction of the conduit began in 1245 and the course, which was extended over the years, ran from Tyburn (north of Oxford Street) eastwards to Charing Cross, along the Strand and Fleet Street into the City via Ludgate.

The conduit was later extended to natural springs at Paddington, accounting for several street names such as Conduit Court, Conduit Place, and Conduit Passage. John Stow described it as consisting of a stone tower, decorated with images of St. Christopher on the top, and angels round about, with 'sweet-sounding bells'. Householders secretly and illegally tapped into the pipe to gain access to water for their own use. In 1478 a brewer, William Campion, siphoned off water from the conduit to his home, for which he was made to parade around publicly on a horse with a vessel of water on his head.

Fleet Street had accumulated innumerable courts, alleys, and bystreets. Until at least the fifteenth century there was a preponderance of hatters and alehouses. Many of the alehouses were run by ale-wives or brewsters and the trade was generally held in low esteem. Many notorious and disorderly taverns abounded and all kinds of vice was rife. In the mid-sixteenth century there were no fewer than twenty-six taverns in St. Dunstan's parish and Alsatia alone.

ALSATIA

Alsatia was the name given in the seventeenth century to the area that covered the present Whitefriars Street, Bouverie Street and the Thames. Carmelite Friars had occupied the area from the reign of Edward I (1272-1307). The religious order began to prosper and this was reflected in the wealth, size, and extent of their buildings. The precincts of the Carmelites were one of the last places of sanctuary in England in 1697. Given the numbers of rogues and criminals who inhabited Alsatia it was not surprising that appeals for sanctuary were common. On many occasions wanted posters were circulated and rewards offered for escaped criminals or dissenters. One such dissenter was Daniel Defoe (1659-1731) who sought sanctuary in Alsatia after writing seditious material against the government. As with so many religious houses, the Carmelite order fell victim to the Reformation during the reign of Henry VIII and from there on the area deteriorated into one of the most notorious places of lawlessness in London.

The notorious Ram Alley, now Hare Place, epitomised all that was dreadful about Alsatia with its reeking dens, unlicensed dram shops, broken gutters, dilapidated house fronts, and its bawds. Ram Alley was also noted for its many cooks who supplied dinners for the neighbouring taverns. In the play, *New Ways to Pay Old Debts* (1625), the dramatist Philip Massinger alluded to this practice:

> The knave thinks still he's at the Cook's shop in Ram Alley,
> Where the clerks divide and the elder is to chose;
> And feeds so slovenly!

Ben Jonson's comedy, *Staple of News* (1626) comments:

> And though Ram Alley stinks with cooks and ale.
> Yet say there's many a worthy lawyer's chamber
> Buts upon Ram Alley

Slinging rubbish and human waste into the street was common practice and the narrow passages and alleys were places where pedestrians often found themselves bespattered, or even drenched, in all sorts of unpleasant refuse hurled from upper windows. In 1638, widow Wall was typical of many who were presented before the courts for throwing the contents of chamber pots out of her windows. Even by the early nineteenth century Ram Alley was still described as being in a ruinous condition.

Another place of ill repute in Alsatia was Hanging Sword Alley, by the side of Whitefriars Lane. The name derives from a house sign mentioned in 1564, when the area was once known for its fencing schools. The alley was also referred to as Blood Bowl Alley, after a notorious night cellar depicted by William Hogarth (1697-1764). Hogarth's illustration, *Industry and Idleness* (1747), depicts variously the body of a murdered man being thrust through a trap door, a fight, and thieves looking at their ill-gotten gains. Hanging Sword Alley also features in *A Tale of Two Cities* (1859) by Charles Dickens (1812-1870) where it is the home of Jerry Cruncher, a porter who earns extra money as a 'resurrection man', removing bodies from their graves for sale to medical schools: 'Mr. Cruncher's apartments were not in a savoury neighbourhood,

Whitefriars Crypt visible from Magpie Alley

and were but two in number, even if a closet with a single pane of glass in it might be counted as one.'

As the reputation of Alsatia declined, a notable industry was established near Temple Lane, which existed for over two centuries. This was the Whitefriars Glass Works founded in 1680. The glassworks changed hands several times before James Powell, a famous wine merchant, bought the works in 1834. The company moved out of Fleet Street to Wealdstone in 1923. The original name of Whitefriars was not reverted back until 1963.

A transformation around what was Alsatia took place in the late nineteenth century when the City authorities established a freehold estate of the area making it attractive to newspaper offices such as the *Daily Mail, Daily Mirror, Evening Standard, News of the World, News Chronicle* and the *Observer*. The changing face of Fleet Street would now be reflected in the businesses and buildings that produced the great output of words.

Why the name Alsatia? The name is thought to be a cant term (thieves' language) for the area. It was taken from the ancient name for Alsace on the French/German border, which was also outside both legislative and judicial supervision. Although many notable inns and alehouses grew up around Alsatia, little now remains of this once notorious area.

However there is a significant reminder of medieval Fleet Street. This is the old White Friars church crypt that was discovered during demolition and can be seen by going down Bouverie Street and turning left into Magpie Alley. The crypt, which stood beneath the lodgings of the prior, was unearthed during building works in 1895. It was cleared and restored in the 1920s when this area was redeveloped on behalf of the *News of the World* newspaper. Further developments took place in the 1980s. The crypt, which originally stood on the east side of the site, was raised onto a concrete raft and moved to its present location. It is possible to view the crypt from outside the building although there is no direct public access to it.

In 1665 the Great Plague, identified as bubonic plague, killed an estimated twenty per cent of London's population. It was the last major outbreak of the plague in England, and the first since 1636. The Plague of 1665 visited the parish of St. Bride's and typically most of the lawyers, merchants, doctors, and other 'well-to-do' people who lived in the area showed their instinct for survival and fled. The poor stayed behind in their crowded alleys and courts leaving themselves vulnerable to the ravages of the plague, thus reinforcing the term 'the Poore's Plague'.

The first case in Fleet Street is recorded on 10 July 1665 in Shoe Lane when a man was suddenly struck down. Other entries began to mount up, with each one making the briefest comment on the passing of a life:

2 August, Elizabeth Roper and her child
15 August, A maid in Piggot's house
19 September, Mrs. Pearson and her child
29 September, A maid from the Crowne in Fleet Street

As news of the disease spread, most clergy abandoned their flock although the ministers of St. Bride's and St. Dunstan's stayed and continued to serve, such as Richard Preston, curate of St. Bride, who witnessed the dreadful devastation to his parish including the deaths of his churchwardens.

The awful catastrophe suddenly created a whole layer of jobs for those who tried to deal with the victims such as 'Searchers of the Dead', who were paid to go out and inspect a corpse to determine the cause of death. There were also dog-killers who culled dogs because they were thought to spread the pestilence; 'rakers' who carried away the corpses; 'bearers' who carried the corpses to the plague pits, and 'brokers of the dead' who seized the property left in infected houses. It was thought that fire would purify the air, and kill the contagion hence bonfires were piled high and blazed day and night in front of Clifford's Inn. The parish lost 2,111 people from the plague in 1665. Sadly this was not the end as Londoners faced further disaster the following year.

The Great Fire of London began on Sunday 2 September 1666 and destroyed 87 City churches as well as the old medieval church of St. Bride's, which was among the fifty-one to be rebuilt. By 4 September the fire reached St. Bride's. The fire engine that the church had acquired had been the victim of neglect and proved to be hopeless in dealing with the flames.

Fleet Street consisted of medieval and Tudor timber buildings, which were helpless against the flames. The poor of Alsatia were driven out as the fire made short work of their hovels. John Evelyn (1620-1706) entered in his diary, 'All Fleet Street, the Old Bailey, Ludgate Hill . . . now flaming and most of it reduced to ashes.' Seamen from the Royal Dockyard at Deptford, who were brought in to help, advised blowing up the houses so as to quell the flames.

All the buildings between St. Dunstan's Church and Temple Bar were saved. To the south of Fleet Street the fire burned down to the Thames leaving little of the Inner Temple standing. There were few deaths recorded around the area of Fleet River but

Statue of Queen Elizabeth at St. Dunstan's Church

to the south of Fleet Street and Ludgate Hill casualty figures were as high as seventy per cent.

At the outbreak of the fire, guards were stationed at certain points in an attempt to prevent the spread of the flames, and to protect property. On 3 September 1666, constables were ordered to keep post around Temple Bar, Clifford's Inn Garden, Fetter Lane, Shoe Lane, and Cow Lane. By the third day of the fire Samuel Pepys saw the flames 'running down to Fleet Street'. At five o'clock in the afternoon the fire had reached the Conduit near Shoe Lane. Pepys wrote on 7 September:

> Up by five o'clock; and blessed be God! I find all well; and by water to Paul's Wharf. Walked thence, and saw all the town burned; and a miserable sight of Paul's church, with all the roof fallen, and the body of the quire fallen into St Fayth's; Paul's School also, Ludgate and Fleet Street, my father's house (in Salisbury Court) and the church (St. Bride's), and a good part of the Temple the like.

There has been a general belief that the Great Fire took few lives, but this is disputed. John Evelyn commented that he noticed in the heat, the stench of the bodies of many people. In Shoe Lane, eighty-year old Paul Lowell, a watchmaker, refused to leave his home and paid the price; his remains were found in the ruins. The statue of Queen

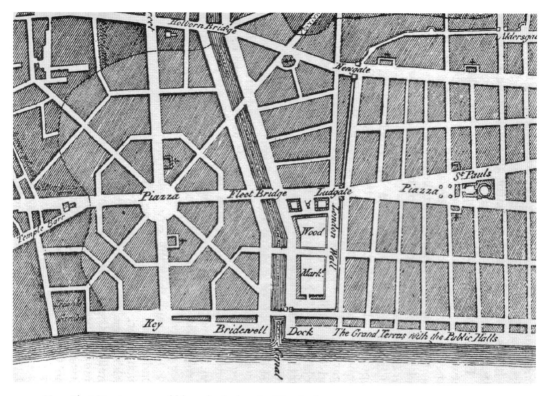

How Fleet Street area would have looked under Wren's plan

Elizabeth, which was made by William Kirwan around 1586, now stands in the wall at St. Dunstan's Church above the vestry porch. It is the only fragment of old Ludgate that survived the fire.

The Great Fire devastated London and precipitated a huge rebuilding of the City. The west part of Fleet Street had succumbed to the flames but as the fire reached St. Dunstan's the brick walls managed to prevent further damage and the fire began to subside. Although many local landmarks and ancient buildings had been consumed by the devastation, the fire prompted the authorities to make the street east of St. Dunstan's towards Ludgate Circus much wider.

On Wren's Plan for the rebuilding of London it was intended that Fleet Street would be ninety feet wide, making for a very large thoroughfare extending from Temple Bar to Tower Hill. The centre of Fleet Street would have included a circus, from which eight subsidiary streets would have branched off. The scheme of course never materialized. An act of the Common Council of 29 April 1667 ordered that Fleet Street be widened from the 'Greyhound Tavern to Ludgate' to a uniform width of forty five feet and certain houses to be set back. Three years later the streets were paved.

The rebuilding of the City was done with remarkable speed. This was particularly so with Fleet Street. The new gateway at Temple Bar was constructed, churches were restored or rebuilt and a new and smaller Bridewell replaced the old Palace. However, the old pockets of vice and crime settled back and continued in their old ways.

TEMPLE BAR

Although Fleet Street is now situated in the ward of Farringdon Without (the largest of the twenty-five City wards), which covers the area east of Chancery Lane, it was not always within the jurisdiction of the City. Most of this area, extending to what is now Farringdon Street, had been in the bounds of the City of Westminster. The old London Wall once defined the boundaries of the City but these expanded over time. During the medieval period the boundaries were extended from Ludgate to Temple Bar, as were other 'City bars' (or barriers), such as at Holborn, Aldersgate, Bishopsgate and Aldgate.

Why and when the area of Fleet Street became part of the jurisdiction of the City is uncertain. The authority of the City of London Corporation had, by the Middle Ages, reached beyond the ancient wall in several places (the Liberties). In order to regulate and protect trade into the City, trade barriers were erected on the main roads. The most famous of these barriers was Temple Bar at the west end of Fleet Street, so named after the Temple Church. A bar is first mentioned here in 1293, although this was little more than a chain or bar between two wooden posts. John Norden in his *Speculum Britannia* (1593) noted that in 1381 on the occasion of Wat Tyler's (1341-1381) Rebellion that the gate 'was thrown down by the Kentish rebels'. This suggests that the Bar was little more than a gate. Outcasts and lepers, forbidden to live in the City, crowded the area around Temple Bar, making it intimidating by their begging and displaying of their sores.

The structure of the Bar seems to have improved by the sixteenth century as John Stow tells us that it was newly painted and repaired. When Philip of Spain arrived in London in 1554 'a good and substantial new pair of gates' was ordered for the occasion. The Bar's demarcation of the entry into the City gave it significance and it is mentioned with regard to receiving the marriage of Mary Tudor to Phillip of Spain and the funeral cortege of Henry VII's Queen, Elizabeth of York. The triumphal procession of Elizabeth I after the defeat of the Spanish Armada (1588) was an occasion when Temple Bar was suitably decorated with City minstrels congregated on the top as she stayed for a while beneath the archway. Elizabeth had stopped to meet the Lord Mayor who presented her with the keys of the City, which she reciprocated by presenting the Lord Mayor with a pearl encrusted sword (one of five City swords) thus establishing a tradition that has continued ever since.

Inigo Jones (1573-1652), the great architect, was invited to design a new archway but the scheme was never carried out. In 1666 the Great Fire had stopped before it reached Temple Bar. Nonetheless the fire had necessitated the rebuilding of much of the City, and the Bar was in a state of disrepair. In July 1669 the Commissioners of Streets and Sewers proposed the removal of the old Temple Bar in order to enlarge the street. Money was raised that contributed to the building of a new Temple Bar.

Sir Christopher Wren reputedly designed the new Portland stone structure, completed in 1672 at a total cost of £1500. We say reputedly because no surviving documents exist to prove that he did, although his son retained original drawings for the work. When completed, the structure bore, on its east side, the following inscription: 'Erected in the year 1670, Sir Samuel Starling, Mayor; continued in the year 1671, Sir Richard Ford, Lord Mayor; and finished in the year 1672, Sir George Waterman, Lord Mayor.' This inscription became, over time, illegible.

Above: *Temple Bar in the late eighteenth century from a drawing by J. A. Archer*

Opposite: *Temple Bar on Fleet Street erected in 1880 to replace old gated arch*

To emphasise the fact that it was a regal monument, it had two stone statues of the east side of the gateway of Queen Anne of Denmark and James I and on the west side were the statues of Charles I and Charles II. Over the keystone on the east side were the City arms.

Among the less decorative ornamentations that were often placed on Temple Bar were the heads and limbs of those executed for high treason. This practice developed after the Rye House Plot of 1683 when a conspiracy to assassinate King Charles II and his brother James, Duke of York was detected. One of the plotters, Sir Thomas Armstrong, was executed and had his limbs exhibited on Temple Bar. Years later, the head and quarters of Sir William Perkins, and the quarters of Sir John Friend, who were both implicated in the plot to assassinate William III, were set up on Temple Bar. In 1716 Colonel Henry Oxburg, a Jacobite supporter, had his head placed on a spike there. However the head of Christopher Layer, in 1723, holds an unenviable record. It was believed that it remained on display for thirty years before being blown down in a gale. Among the last victims to be exhibited were those who suffered for their complicity in the 1745 Jacobite Rebellion. The body parts of Francis Towneley and George Fletcher were set up in 1746 and among the more macabre commercial activities of eighteenth century London was that of letting spyglasses out at a halfpenny a look.

The gates were once closed during the 'Wilkes and Liberty' riots (see Riots, Brawls and Pillory chapter) in 1769 when some 600 merchants, bankers, and others opposing John Wilkes, set out from the City to present an address to the King. However, the mob had closed the gates by force thus preventing the deputation from proceeding. Not to be deterred, about 150 of the opponents managed to proceed up Chancery Lane and other indirect routes, and duly presented their address.

As the local population and the traffic grew during the nineteenth century, the Strand and Fleet Street became increasingly congested and it was decided in 1878, after 200 years, to remove Temple Bar. The City of London Corporation was keen to widen the road but did not want to destroy the historic monument so it was dismantled stone by stone in the hope that it might be erected elsewhere. That elsewhere came in 1880, when the brewer Sir Henry Meux bought the stones with the intention of reconstructing the Bar as a gateway to his park and mansion at Theobalds Park, Cheshunt in Hertfordshire. Having witnessed so many eventful occasions, Temple Bar now stood in retirement in tranquil woodland surroundings.

With the important ceremonial entrance to the City of London from Westminster now removed, would another structure replace it, and if so where would it be sited? The Attorney General was asked in the House of Commons in August 1880 if he was aware, that 'the Corporation of London are now preparing to erect, in the centre of one of the busiest parts of Fleet Street, an edifice to commemorate the site of Temple Bar'. Mr. Firth, the questioner, also raised the issue as to whether such a monument would cause an obstruction. Sir Henry James, the Attorney General, stated that the 'Corporation intended to erect a refuge in the centre of the roadway where Temple Bar was formerly situated, and the effect would be that the roadway would form two roads 17 feet 2 inches wide'.

The monument, which still stands in the middle of the road opposite the Law Courts where Fleet Street takes over from the Strand, marks the place of the old Temple Bar. The architect Sir Horace Jones designed the new Temple Bar, and the heraldic bronze griffin (a legendary monster and emblem of the City of London) on the top is by the sculptor Charles Bell Birch (1832-1893), whilst the bronze freestanding statues of Queen Victoria and the Prince of Wales are by Sir Joseph Boehm. The new Bar was not to everyone's liking. London historian Beresford Chancellor commented that 'the removal of Temple Bar and the substitution of the ridiculous Griffin has taken from it its most picturesque landmark and added its most useless feature'.

Meanwhile the old Temple Bar gradually became dilapidated over the years and in 1976 the Temple Bar Trust was established with the intention of returning the Bar to the City of London. Twenty-eight years later, with financial contributions from the Corporation of London, the Temple Bar Trust, and several Livery Companies, the Temple Bar came home. In November 2004 the old Temple Bar was officially opened by the Lord Mayor, in its new position adjacent to the northwest tower of St Paul's Cathedral. It now forms a pedestrian gateway into the redeveloped Paternoster Square.

Opposite: *The old Temple Bar that now stands in Paternoster Square opposite St Paul's Cathedral*

CHAPTER FOUR

BUILDINGS OF FLEET STREET

It would be impossible to do justice to so many buildings in and around Fleet Street that have come and gone as well as remained over the centuries. As a number of houses, inns and churches are covered in other parts of the book, this chapter will be selective in its choice of buildings.

An appropriate start is No. 1 Fleet Street at the Strand end. The Royal Bank of Scotland now occupies the site where two famous buildings once stood: The Devil Tavern and Child's Bank. Child & Co. is the oldest banking house in London dating back to the late 17th century. It was named after Francis Child, a London goldsmith, who entered into partnership with Robert Blanchard in 1664. Child's Bank issued the first banknotes in London in 1729. The business thrived and was appointed the 'jeweller in ordinary' to King William III (r.1689-1702). The bank acquired the adjoining old Devil Tavern, and erected a new block of houses, and it was here that the bank became famous.

The bank's proximity to the Inns of Court attracted many customers from among the legal profession, and links were also developed with a number of Oxford colleges. When Temple Bar was removed and the street widened, Child & Co. built an elegant new banking house that opened in 1880. In 1923 the bank was sold to Glyn, Mills, Currie, Holt & Co., which was in turn bought by the Royal Bank of Scotland (RBS) in 1939. The RBS retained Child & Co. as a separate business, which continues to this day at No. 1, Fleet Street. Child's was described by Charles Dickens in *A Tale of Two Cities* (1859) as: 'an old-fashioned place, moreover, in the moral attribute that the partners in the House were proud of its smallness, proud of its darkness, proud of its ugliness, proud of its incommodiousness.'

Another famous bank is Hoare's, which stands at No. 37 Fleet Street and is England's oldest privately owned bank. Richard Hoare (1648-1719) founded it in 1672 at the sign of the Golden Bottle (a gilded leather bottle that hung outside the shop) in Cheapside, and in 1690 he moved the business to new premises in Fleet Street along with the Golden Bottle. Among its famous customers were Catherine of Braganza (wife of King Charles II), Samuel Pepys and John Dryden. The bank prospered during the eighteenth century; Richard Hoare was knighted in 1702 then became Lord Mayor in 1712. After his death his two sons, Henry and Benjamin, continued the business. It was his grandson Henry Hoare who dominated the family through his wealth and personality. Hoare's Bank gradually introduced many aspects of modern banking including the first cheques in March 1763.

No. 1 Fleet Street, the site of the Devil Tavern, *demolished in 1787, and where the Royal Bank of Scotland now stands.*

In 1829 the premises at Fleet Street were rebuilt and it continued to have famous customers including Lord Byron and Jane Austen. Following the Bank Charter Act 1833, many of the 4,000 or so private banks disappeared, but Hoare's maintained a steady business until it experienced a period of unsuccessful speculation and poor management in the second half of the nineteenth century. After the First World War the larger banks absorbed most of the remaining private banks but Hoare's decided not to merge and still remains an independent bank.

Near to Hoare's Bank is the handsome Wren gateway to Middle Temple, with the image of a carved sheep above the door dating from 1684, whilst the timber-framed Prince Henry Rooms are at No. 17. This building is one of the few timbered houses to survive the Great Fire and Second World War bombers. However, the exterior was rebuilt in the twentieth century. It is named after Prince Henry (elder son of King James I), who would have become King Henry IX had he not died of typhoid at the age of eighteen in 1612.

The history of the site can be traced back to the 12th century when it formed part of the property granted to the Knights Templar. At the beginning of the sixteenth century tenants included the landlord of an inn called *The Hand*. In 1610 the property was rebuilt and it became a tavern known for the next thirty years as the *Prince's Arms*. It was sold in 1671 to James Sotheby in whose family the freehold remained until the London County Council bought it in 1900. The house changed its name to the Fountain

Above: *Hoare's Bank, England's oldest privately owned bank*

Right: *Wren's gateway to the Middle Temple*

during the seventeenth century and from 1795 to 1816 Mrs. Salmon's Waxworks occupied the front part of the house while the tavern continued its business at the rear of the premises.

A number of stories surround the site. For example when the London County Council took over the building, a signboard across the front declared that it was 'formerly the palace of Henry VIII and Cardinal Wolsey'. However, evidence of the rebuilding in 1610 refutes this claim. Another story suggests that the house was built for the Council of the Duchy of Cornwall, and that the room on the first floor was used by Prince Henry after he became Prince of Wales in 1610. This might explain the three feathers motif on the façade, and why the inn was called The Prince's Arms, but records show that the house was erected as a tavern and that the name was in use two years before Prince Henry was born.

A discovery in 1900 revealed that there was a false front on the building incorporating eight carved panels, but behind this was the original seventeenth-century half-timbered front, entirely preserved by the thick layers of paint that covered the whole front. The façade now appears in its original form.

Opened in 1975, the Prince Henry Rooms contain one of the best remaining Jacobean enriched plaster ceilings in London, as well as contemporary items, prints, and paintings depicting the diarist Samuel Pepys. The main feature in the interior is the large room on the first floor. It was originally panelled in oak, but only a section on the west side of the room now remains. The remaining panelling and the chimneypiece are Georgian. There are two twentieth-century stained glass windows in the room. The right-hand window is the 'Royal' window, which commemorates the supposed association with the Duchy of Cornwall, whilst the other window illustrates the connection of the room with the London County Council, the City of London, and the Society of the Inner Temple.

Close to the Prince Henry Rooms is Goslings Bank, established in 1650 at the 'Sign of Ye Three Squirrels', a hanging signboard depicting three squirrels that still hangs there. After becoming Goslings and Sharpe, it was a constituent bank in the Barclays & Co. merger of 1896 but is still known as Gosling's Branch. The site is now located at No. 19 Fleet Street. The founders of the three banking houses in Fleet Street – the Childs, the Hoares, and the Goslings, were all, at various times, aldermen of this ward.

At the far north east end on the eastern bank of Farringdon Street was the site of Fleet Prison. A notorious gaol, it was built in 1197 but was destroyed during the Peasant's Revolt of 1381. It was destroyed and rebuilt on two further occasions including the following of the Great Fire of 1666. Fleet Prison had established a reputation in the eighteenth century as a place for debtors and contained about 300 prisoners and their families. It was not uncommon for inmates to beg for alms from passers-by in order to pay for their keep. They did this from a grille built into the wall on the Farringdon Street side of the prison. As prisons were privately owned, profit-making enterprises, those incarcerated had to pay for food and lodging.

The head of the prison, the warden, was appointed by patent and it became a frequent practice of the holder of the patent to 'farm out' the prison to the highest bidder. This custom made Fleet Prison notorious for the cruelties inflicted on prisoners. One purchaser of the office was Thomas Bambridge, an infamous warden of particularly evil repute, who in 1728 paid, with another man, the sum of £3000 to John Huggins for the wardenship. Bambridge was guilty of many great extortions upon prisoners and, in the words of a committee of the House of Commons appointed to inquire into the state of the gaols of the kingdom, 'arbitrarily and unlawfully loaded with irons, put into

The distinctive Prince Henry's House

The sign of the Three Squirrels that denoted Goslings Bank

dungeons, and destroyed prisoners for debt, treating them in the most barbarous and cruel manner'. He was committed to Newgate, and an act was passed to prevent his enjoying the office of warden, or any other office whatsoever. Nonetheless his time in Newgate was short, and he was allowed to have prostitutes visit him frequently. He was acquitted at his trial at the Old Bailey in 1729.

Prisoners of the Fleet could take lodgings close to the prison as long as they paid the keeper to compensate him for loss of earnings. The area in which prisoners could exercise this privilege was known as the Liberty of the Fleet, which also became known for its quickie weddings.

A Fleet Marriage was the best-known example of a clandestine or irregular marriage taking place in England before the Marriage Act 1753. Such marriages at the Fleet date back to 1613. An irregular marriage took place away from the home parish of the spouses, whilst clandestine marriages had an element of secrecy to them. For example no parental consent was required and no questions of bigamy were involved. These types of marriage involved a fee for the service, which was often undertaken by disgraced clergymen unscrupulous enough to conduct these ceremonies. Such marriages were so popular that in the 1740s over 6000 marriages annually were taking place in the environs of the Fleet Prison.

It was because of the abuses brought about by clandestine marriages that the 1753 Marriage Act was passed. The Act, which effectively put a stop to these marriages in England, required that banns should be published or a licence obtained and that the marriage should be solemnised in church. As for the Fleet Prison, this was finally closed in 1844 and sold to the corporation of the City of London, by whom it was pulled down in 1846.

Depiction of a Fleet Marriage

Inside the Bridewell

One of the most historic buildings was the ancient palace of Bridewell, which, after having served its original regal purpose, was put to a very different use and eventually disappeared. It stood on a vast site along the western bank of the Fleet River, reaching up from the Thames to the present day Fleet Street. A royal residence had been situated at this spot from the earliest times. It is believed that the Norman kings once held their courts at Bridewell Palace, and King Henry I (r. 1100-1135) is reported to have given stone for an early rebuilding of the palace. However, the first clear reference to the building is in 1522 when Emperor Charles V came to England and Henry VIII ordered that the palace be built for his accommodation. In fact, Charles V did not stay there; he chose Blackfriars instead. Nonetheless his attendants did take up residence in Bridewell. Henry VIII frequently used Bridewell, and stayed here in 1525, when his Parliament was held in the hall of Blackfriars.

After the death of King Henry VIII in 1547 the palace was left deserted and in 1553, according to John Stow, King Edward VI (r. 1547-1553) gave the palace for 'the commonalty and citizens, to be a workhouse for the poor and idle persons of the City'. However, as with so many charitable gifts, it fell victim to fraud. A major problem was that the Bridewell had not been sufficiently endowed, so it became a serious expense and burden to the citizens.

Before the fire of 1666, Bridewell extended from half way up Bridge Street to the water's edge. When it was rebuilt in 1668 the new structure only covered about half of the previous space. The old palace now had the dual object of incarcerating disorderly and idle persons, and receiving the needy and helpless. In his two-volume work *New View of London* (1708), Edward Hatton described the Bridewell as

. . . a prison and house of correction for idle vagrants, loose and disorderly servants, night-walkers, etc. These are set to hard labour, and have correction according to their deserts; but have their clothes and diet during their imprisonment at the charge of the house. It is also a hospital for indigent persons.

Bridewell appears often in eighteenth century literature, and is associated with flogging, beating hemp and oakum-picking, which were the chief punishments. Hogarth depicted the interior of Bridewell in the fourth plate of *The Harlot's Progress* (1732) where the central character Moll has been sentenced to hard labour, beating hemp with a mallet, a process used for producing rope. The plate shows the prison warder directing her to continue working, while his one-eyed wife steals a bit of Moll's lace collar from her dress. Hogarth, in typical fashion, shows all manner of impoverished and depraved humanity, swept up and left to the mercy of cruel warders and the meaningless system of so-called correction.

Bridewell later became united with Bethlehem Hospital and the House of Occupation. In 1842 there were 1324 persons confined there. Contemporaries consistently noted how bad the building was, stating that 'it stands upon a cold damp soil, [and] is far from healthy'. When Holloway Prison was built in 1863, and the materials of Bridewell sold, London saw the end of an institution that had given its name to similar places of confinement and correction. The name Bridewell continues today only as the Bridewell Theatre on Bride Lane.

Opposite: *The Bridewell Theatre on Bride Lane*

CHAPTER FIVE

BRAWLS, RIOTS AND PUNISHMENTS

London has a long tradition of rioting and violence. Fleet Street, as a main thoroughfare between the City and Westminster, witnessed many such events, and contributed to London's role in the bloody history of protest, riot, and punishment. The presence of a large number of taverns contributed to this state of affairs, as did the inadequate means of policing the streets. Such was the concern about the riotous nature of the inns that in 1629 the Lords of the Council wrote to the Lord Mayor requesting him 'to shut up the taverns in Fleet Street from which the persons who caused the tumults there came; and to commit the masters of such taverns to the houses of such citizens as he should think fit'.

Chronicles of the Middle Ages tell us of much blood being spilt and many acts of violence committed. In 1307 the priory of the White Friars was broken into with the aid and connivance of one of the friars, whose assistance helped the robbers to get away with 40 lbs of silver. In the process of their robbery, they bound the hands of the Prior and killed one of the friars. The friar, who had been complicit, was later arrested and hanged. In 1311, five members of King Edward II's (r.1307-1327) household were arrested in Fleet Street for a burglary. The King demanded they be released, but the City refused to give them up. In 1338 some of the Carmelite friars had clearly descended into such sinful and dissolute ways that King Edward III (r.1327-1377) found it necessary to threaten them with arrest and appropriate punishment. In Richard II's reign (1377-1399), Wat Tyler's fierce Kentish men sacked the Savoy church (part of the Temple) and destroyed two forges, which had been originally erected on each side of St. Dunstan's church by the Knights Templar. In 1440, Londoner's witnessed an unusual procession when Eleanor Cobham, Duchess of Gloucester, did penance through Fleet Street for practicing witchcraft against the King. The following year, a fight between gangs of locals and young men from the Inns of Court lasted for two days.

In 1458 a more serious riot occurred when law students were driven back (some were killed) by archers who fired on them from the Conduit near Shoe Lane. Fights and street brawls were commonplace, and passers-by ran the risk of being attacked. The diarist Henry Machyn recorded in 1559 that there was a great fray in Fleet Street between five and seven at night in which one man had his nose cut off. A street fight in 1570 in Fleet Street resulted in three watchmen being so injured that it was recorded that they would 'likely to be cripples for ever'.

It seems that the London apprentices were never far from disturbances, and they often gave cause for alarm. In 1621, three apprentices abused the Spanish ambassador as he passed their master's door in Fenchurch Street. The King ordered the riotous youths to be whipped from Aldgate to Temple Bar. In an act of solidarity, fellow apprentices came out in force in Fleet Street, released the lads and then started to beat up the officer accompanying them. Seven years later a festival turned into a brawl and four people lost their lives. Two of the rioters were arrested and subsequently executed.

Eight years later in 1629, what started as an arrest of some rioters in Fleet Street quickly developed into scuffles between army officers and a mob that had suddenly appeared from nearby taverns. A Captain Dawson and two other officers were killed, and several wounded. The Lord Mayor ordered all the taverns on Fleet Street to be closed for three weeks.

The constantly busy thoroughfare of Fleet Street saw many prisoners paraded along this route to suffer punishment. The radical John Lilburne (1615-1657), a leading spokesman for the Levellers in the Civil War, was found guilty of contempt in 1638 for printing and distributing unlicensed Puritan books and pamphlets in London. He obstinately refused to take the oath, and claimed that his prosecution was unlawful. Nonetheless he was stripped to the waist, tied to the back of a cart and taken slowly down Fleet Street, through Temple Bar, into the Strand and on to Charing Cross. Lilburne loudly declared that he had committed no crime against the law or the state and that he was a victim of the bishops' cruelty. During the journey Lilburne received 500 lashes but supportive crowds who had lined the route, cheered the defiant man.

Street brawls were commonplace and Ned Ward recorded many of these in his *London Spy* during the 1690s as he walked along Fleet Street.

> Just as we passed by, a feud was kindling between two rival females. These, from the brimstone of lust, had blown up such a fire of jealousy between 'em that the one called the other an adulterous bitch, and charged her with lying with her husband and robbing her of her love . . . Then with teeth and nails she made a violent assault on her rival, who roared out for help, crying that she was quick with child.

On this occasion the mob, sympathising with the pregnant woman, intervened and pulled the women apart.

The so called 'Alsatians', the troublesome elements who lived in the area that became known for a brief period as Alsatia, often caused fights, particularly with the benchers – student barristers of the Inner Temple. In July 1691, weary of their riotous and thieving neighbours, the benchers bricked up the gate leading into the high street of Whitefriars. Seeing this as a challenge, the Alsatians quickly pulled it down. The benchers regrouped and drew their swords, to which the Alsatians responded with pokers and shovels. A melee ensued where many heads were broken, several people were wounded, many hurried off to prison and two men were killed. The ringleader of the Alsatians, Francis White, was convicted of murder in April 1693.

The riots in Alsatia were depicted in Sir Walter Scott's novel, *The Fortunes of Nigel* (1822). Set in the early seventeenth century, Scott portrays Alsatia in atmospheric style with its foggy, dingy, crowded streets eastward of the Temple, which became a sanctuary for the eponymous Nigel, who lives among the ruffians and thieves. It is in this dreadful environment where

Seventeenth-century street brawl

The wailing of children, the scolding of their mothers, the miserable exhibition of ragged linen hung from the windows to dry, spoke the wants and distresses of the wretched inhabitants; while the sounds of complaint were mocked and overwhelmed by the riotous shouts, oaths, profane songs, and boisterous laughter that issued from the alehouses and taverns, which, as the signs indicated, were equal in number to all the other houses.

However, it was Thomas Shadwell (1642-1692) who was the first author to make literary use of the area in his play the *Squire of Alsatia* (1688). Shadwell portrayed the type of people that populated Alsatia: degraded clergymen who married anybody for five shillings, broken lawyers, skulking bankrupts, sullen homicides, thievish money-lenders, and gaudy courtesans. In one scene Sir William Belfond, an old country gentleman, comes to confront his son during his disgraceful revels at the George Tavern in Bouverie Street. Four villains shout, 'An arrest! an arrest! A bailiff! a bailiff!' All the scum of Alsatia chase the old gentleman before he emerges into Fleet Street, hot, battered, and bruised. The message is clear: don't threaten the privileges of Whitefriars. However, the riots of 1691 did threaten their privileges because they led to the abolition of London's criminal sanctuaries.

In March 1710, the Sacheverell riots erupted in London's West End following the impeachment of Dr Henry Sacheverell, an Anglican Oxford don. Sacheverell was tried at Westminster Hall for publishing a sermon condemning the Whig government for its favouritism towards dissenters. Rioters demonstrated their sympathy for the doctor by sacking and burning six prominent dissenting chapels. Among these was the chapel of the United Brethren, or Moravians, in Fetter Lane. This chapel was dismantled along with other chapels in the area. After carrying Dr. Sacheverell in triumph to his lodgings in the Temple, the mob, who had already torn up the benches and pulpits of several churches, made a bonfire in Lincoln's Inn Fields, and danced with shouts of 'High Church and Sacheverell.'

Pointless violence was a characteristic of the Mohocks, a gang that terrorised London in the early eighteenth century, attacking men and women alike. Events came to a head in 1712 when a bounty was issued by the royal court for the capture of the so-called Mohocks. They were reputed to be yobbish gentlemen, possibly because they did not take any money from anyone, although their violence included attacking and disfiguring innocent people. Their activities stretched as far as Fleet Street, where they 'boxed the Charlies, broke windows, and stole knockers.' John Addison, (1672-1719), essayist, poet, and politician confirmed these fears in the *Spectator* in 1712 when he was asked whether he felt in danger in case the Mohocks should be lurking.

> I assure you I thought I had fallen into their Hands last Night; for I observed two or three lusty black Men that followed me half way up Fleet-street, and mended their pace behind me, in proportion as I put on to get away from them . . . I fancied they had a mind to hunt me.

On another occasion in the same year he walked along Fleet Street,

> and having, out of curiosity, just entered into Discourse with a wandering Female who was travelling the same Way, a couple of Fellows advanced towards us and drew their Swords . . . I made a handsome and orderly Retreat, having suffered no other Damage in this Action than the Loss of my Baggage.

Another source of riot and disturbance were the Mug House Clubs that existed in London at the beginning of the eighteenth century. They took their name from the mugs that each particular member drank his ale out of. After the death of Queen Anne in 1714 the hopes of the Jacobites (supporters of the restoration of the Catholic Stuarts to the throne) were raised. In an attempt to unite their party and organise places for meetings, the Whigs established the Mug Houses in various parts of the City where they drank toasts, sang loyal songs, and arranged party processions. However these assemblies were not always peaceful affairs and soon led to violent clashes with the Tories. Divisions were marked on the one side by the Tories who would shout 'High Church;' 'Ormond for ever' (after the Jacobite Duke of Ormond);' 'No King George;' 'Down with the Presbyterians;' 'Down with the Mug Houses'. On the other side the Whigs roared 'King George for ever', and displayed orange cockades with the motto, 'With heart and hand, By George we'll stand.'

One of the earliest Mug Houses was in Salisbury Court, and its frequenters were among the noisiest. In July 1716, following an attack on a Mug House in Cheapside, a similar assault took place against the one in Salisbury Court.

The Tories claimed that the Whigs were shouting, 'down with the Church'. This proved too much for the Tories and provided them with an excuse to attack the club.

They threatened to level the house and make a bonfire of the timber in the middle of Fleet Street. The Whigs barricaded the door and sent a messenger through the rear entrance to get reinforcements. Eventually a gang of Whigs arrived wielding bludgeons, which encouraged those barricaded inside the club. Fired up by this new support, they then took up pokers, tongs, pitchforks and legs of stools, and sailed into the Tory mob, who soon fled.

Smarting from this, the Tories swore revenge, and a few days later they stormed the club. The *Weekly Journal*, a Whig newspaper, described the Tory mob as High Church chimneysweeps, hackney coachmen, foot-boys, tinkers, shoeblacks, street idlers, ballad singers, and strumpets. The paper on 28 July 1716 added:

> The Papists and Jacobites assembled a mob . . . to attack Mr. Goslin's house, at the sign of the 'Blew Boar's Head,' near Water Lane, in Fleet Street . . . Afterwards they went to the above-said mug-house in Salisbury Court; but the cowardly Jacks not being able to accomplish their hellish designs that night, assembled next day in great numbers from all parts of the town, breaking the windows with brick-bats, broke open the cellar, got into the lower rooms, which they robbed, and pulled down the sign . . . Some of the rioters were desperately wounded, and one Vaughan, a seditious weaver, formerly an apprentice in Bridewell, and since employed there, who was a notorious ringleader of mobs, was killed at the aforesaid mug-house.

At the coroner's inquest of the man killed in Salisbury Court, witnesses said they saw a great many people 'gathered together about the mug-house, throwing stones and dirt'. The mob forced their way into the house and stole money from the till, spilt the beer about the cellar, and 'what goods they could not carry away, they brought into the streets and broke to pieces'. Five of the rioters were eventually hanged at Tyburn, in the presence of a vast crowd.

Nearly fifty years later in June 1762, the MP and radical John Wilkes (1725-1797) established the newspaper *The North Briton*, in which he attacked King George III. The King and his ministers decided to prosecute Wilkes for seditious libel. Wilkes was arrested but he was protected by parliamentary privilege and his discharge was greeted with great popular acclaim. A mob burnt a large jack-boot in the centre of Fleet Street in ridicule of the Prime Minister, Lord Bute. Later that year the House of Commons voted that a member's privilege from arrest did not extend to the writing and publishing of seditious libels. On his return from France in 1768, Wilkes was arrested and during the following weeks a large crowd assembled chanting 'Wilkes and Liberty', 'No Liberty, No King', and 'Damn the King!' Troops turned out in force and opened fire on the crowd, killing seven people. This action sparked further disturbances all over London. The supporters of Wilkes congregated around Temple Bar and closed it in order to block a procession of 600 people who were denouncing Wilkes and the attempts to spread sedition and uproot the constitution. The carriages that accompanied the anti-Wilkites were met with a hail of stones, and the City Marshal, who tried to open the gates, was pelted with mud. Some of the anti-Wilkites took shelter in a nearby coffee house whilst others fled down Chancery Lane. A statue in nearby Fetter Lane commemorates Wilkes.

These riots pale in significance when compared to the Gordon Riots of June 1780, which witnessed massive destruction to property in London, as well as the loss of 290 lives. The riots were the result of the passing of the Catholic Relief Act in 1778, which had attempted to move towards more religious toleration, such as absolving Catholics from taking the religious oath on joining the army. Lord George Gordon (1751-1793), an influential and extreme Protestant, set up the Protestant Association in 1780, demanding the repeal of the Catholic Relief Act. Tapping into an anti-Catholic hostility going back to the sixteenth century, he argued that Roman Catholics in the British army, especially the Irish, might join forces with their French and Spanish co-religionists and attack England. In June 1780, a crowd of some 60,000 marched to the House of Commons to present a petition for the repeal of the Catholic Relief Act, but the situation got completely out of control and the mob took over London for a week. They looted, burned, waved placards, attacked prisons and Catholic churches, and the homes of leading Catholics.

The Gordon Rioters reached Fleet Street on 7 June and headed for the Fleet Prison. That evening they attacked a detachment of Guards in Fleet Street and had to be repelled by bayonet. Twenty men fell and thirty-five were wounded, two of whom died later. The mob returned to set fire to the Fleet prison. A witness to the fire was Fleet street silversmith Joseph Brasbridge, who published his memoirs in *The Fruits Of Experience* (1824). Brasbridge records how he went up to the top of St. Bride's steeple to see the awful spectacle of the conflagration of the Fleet Prison, but the flakes of fire, even at that great height, fell so thickly as to render the situation untenable.

It took a week for the government to collect enough militia and troops to suppress the riots. In the end twenty-five ringleaders were hanged, and Lord George Gordon was indicted for high treason but was found not guilty. His life ended after a number of controversies, notably one surrounding his conversion to Judaism, for which he was ostracised. He died in Newgate Prison in 1793 of typhoid fever.

Over the years many radicals gravitated to Fleet Street where they became residents. In 1834 Richard Carlile (1790-1843), a supporter of the freedom of the press and universal suffrage, exhibited from his shop window on Fleet Street, life-size figures of a jolly fat bishop and a devil linked arm in arm with a placard reading 'Props of the Church'. Crowds flocked to look and laugh at this satirical display, but such subversion and popular support displeased the parish authorities who sent Carlile to prison for three years. His protest had been prompted by church rates that had been levied on his house.

Other radicals included shoemaker Thomas Hardy, who had a shop on the north side of Fleet Street. Hardy was secretary to the London Corresponding Society, which campaigned for parliamentary reform. In the early nineteenth century, pamphleteer and journalist William Cobbett (1763-1835) issued, from 1863 Fleet Street, his weekly *Political Register*, which advocated widening the franchise. It was at the same address in 1851 that the Chartist John James Bezer (1816-88) took over as publisher of the *Christian Socialist*, using the office of the Society for Promoting Working Men's Associations. Here he also published the *Star of Freedom* (previously the famed *Northern Star*). Two great writers, political philosopher Thomas Hobbes (1588-1679) and radical Tom Paine (1737-1809) lived in Fetter Lane, albeit at different times.

Parliamentary reform, and campaigns to extend the vote were notoriously lively and often violent. This was particularly so in the 1830s when pressures to pass the Reform Act became especially volatile. In 1830 large crowds demonstrated in favour of reform although the protests were soon aimed at a range of other grievances. The crowd swelled around the streets of Charing Cross and the Strand shouting 'No Peel', and 'Down with the Lobsters' (the new Metropolitan Police force which had been created by Robert Peel, the Home Secretary, in 1829). By seven o'clock in the evening the vast crowd congregated around Temple Bar. Stones were thrown, and attempts were made to close the gates of the Bar. The City marshals kept the gates open and opposed the passage of the mob to the Strand. Rioters began to pelt the police with stones and pieces of wood broken from the scaffolding of the Law Institute in Chancery Lane. Eventually the crowd was dispersed, although they began to regroup in Bethnal Green, Spitalfields, and Whitechapel.

Among the punishments meted out to tens of thousands of people was transportation overseas, first to America before 1776 and then to Australia between 1787 and 1868. One of many such individuals around Fleet Street who were transported was John Eyre, who lived in Salisbury Court. Eyre was a rich man but was found guilty of stealing paper from the Guildhall in 1771.

In 1790 Maria McKenzie was transported for seven years for stealing a gold watch from Samuel Playsted in Johnson's Court, Fleet Street. In the same year, one James Bond was arrested in a public house in Ram Alley for stealing a coat. He was given seven years transportation. Mary Melling was transported for stealing a watch and keys from William Marks in Fleet Street. In 1813, William Fazakerly stole a number of books from Robert Saunders, who was an auctioneer at 'Poets-Gallery', Fleet Street. These cases represent hundreds of mainly petty criminal offences that went on daily around Fleet Street, and they can be found in the Old Bailey records.

Fleet Street also provided the venue for a number of public executions. Henry Machyn, clothier and seller of funeral trappings, recorded in his dairy in 1555 that a pair of gallows was set up in Fleet Street where two men were hanged and left 'all day in the rain' for the robbery of a Spaniard. At the junction of Fleet Street and Fetter Lane on 4 March 1590 Catholic preacher Christopher Bales was executed for high treason and placed in the gibbet at this junction. Prior to his execution, Bales had been subjected to the agonies of priest hunter Richard Topcliffe, who racked and tortured Bales and hung him up by the hands for twenty-four hours at a time.

In 1607 a strange murder was committed in the Whitefriars area involving Lord Sanquhar, a Scottish nobleman who, with some fellow countrymen, had followed his King, James I (VI) to England. During his time in Whitefriars, Sanquhar had an eye put out by a fencing-master, John Turner. Sanquhar brooded and contemplated revenge and so hired two fellow Scots. In May 1612, about seven o'clock in the evening, the two men went to a tavern in Whitefriars, which Turner often frequented. One of the assassins discharged a pistol into Turner's chest. The murderer was caught later and a reward was issued for the arrest of Sanquhar. On hearing this, he surrendered himself to the Archbishop of Canterbury. Sanquhar was tried in Westminster Hall, and on 29 June he was hanged.

In 1684, John Hutchins, who killed a waterman in Fleet Street, was hanged, despite his denials, on a gibbet erected near the place of the murder. A notorious execution was that of twenty-two year-old Sarah Malcolm, hanged for a triple murder in March 1733 in Old Mitre Court off Fleet Street. Malcolm, a laundress, attacked one of her customers as well as a serving woman and a young girl, and then proceeded to rob the premises. Two days before her execution she sat to be sketched by none other than William Hogarth, 'splendidly dressed in scarlet' just for the occasion. Such was the interest the case generated, that her corpse was put on display and large numbers of people paid good money to view it.

In Joseph Brasbridge's memoirs, *The Fruits Of Experience* (1824), he records how a surgeon who lived at No. 3 Gough Square purchased the body of a Malefactor hanged at Tyburn and brought it to his house. In the evening, his servant-maid, drawn by some morbid curiosity, went to the room where the body had been laid. She was horrified to find the corpse sitting up on the dissecting table. Occasionally, hanged felons did sometimes recover in the anatomy theatre. The surgeon in this case made arrangements for sending the man to America where he succeeded in amassing a fortune, which he bequeathed to his benefactor.

Many places in London witnessed executions and other types of punishment. A popular punishment, at least for the crowd, was the pillory. This consisted of hinged wooden boards that formed holes through which the head and arms were inserted. The boards were then locked together to secure the prisoner. Pillories were set up to hold petty criminals in marketplaces, crossroads, and other public places and sometimes placed on platforms to increase public visibility of the punished offender.

A pillory was set up at Temple Bar in 1670 where the hated Titus Oates stood, amidst showers of bad eggs, dead cats, offal, mud and excrement. Titus Oates (1649-1705) was an Anglican priest who claimed there was a Jesuit-led plan to assassinate Charles II in order to hasten the succession of his Catholic brother James. Oates' story was a complete fabrication, but it was sufficient to create a scare as well as sending a number of innocent men to their deaths at Tyburn. These events sparked a wave of anti-Catholic persecution with thirty-five innocent people executed and hundreds of others suffering as a consequence of Oates' claims. In sentencing Oates' Judge Withers said, 'I never pronounce criminal sentence but with some compassion; but you are such a villain and hardened sinner, that I can find no sentiment of compassion for you.'

Oates was not the only victim to stand in this moveable pillory. In 1671 a man stood upon the pillory at the end of Shoe Lane for insulting Lord Ambassador Coventry. In 1682 George Robinson was convicted of counterfeiting and made to stand in the pillory for two hours in Fleet Street, the Royal Exchange, and in Cheapside. A highwayman, William Davis, better know as the 'Golden Farmer', attempted to seek refuge in Alsatia in 1690, and was made an example of when he was displayed in a gibbet on Fleet Street at the end of Salisbury Court.

In December 1707 *The English Post* reported that, 'last Saturday two more of those Persons that were lately convicted of Unnatural Lewdness were set on the Pillory at Chancery-Lane-end in Fleet-street.' Punishment for the then crime of sodomy was savage and often carried the death penalty. In July 1726 *The London Journal* recorded that Joseph Cuttler was tried and convicted for attempting to extort money from a shopkeeper in Fleet Street. Cuttler had threatened to accuse the man of sodomy if he did not pay. Cuttler was fined, sentenced to suffer six months imprisonment, and to stand in the pillory in Fleet Street, 'over-against Shoe-Lane End'. The outraged crowd who assembled at the pillory pelted him so much with 'Stones and Filth that he bled plentifully, and fainted on the Pillory, before he was carried off for dead'. The *Annual Register* of 25

June 1759 reported that Samuel Scrimshaw and James Ross were convicted for sending threatening letters to Humphrey Morrice with intent to extort money from him. They and two accomplices were sentenced to stand twice in the pillory, once in Cheapside, and once in Fleet Street where they were severely pelted by the populace.

The crowd did not always respond so ferociously to those in the pillory. They could also be remarkably lenient. The *Post Boy* recorded that Tristrum Savage stood in the pillory in June 1702 at the 'Chancery Lane end in Fleet Street, for publishing a scandalous paper, called *The Black List*, and some people had the confidence to give him wine and money as he stood in the pillory'. Celebrated writer Daniel Defoe was sentenced for writing a pamphlet that lampooned the Church. In 1703 he was ordered to stand in the pillory for an hour on three separate days. On the third day he stood in the Fleet Street pillory. The Tories, who were outraged by the pamphlet, claimed that the Whigs had hired a gang to protect Defoe whilst he stood in the pillory. This may be true but it was said that the crowd threw flowers rather than stones and the usual garbage at him because of the respect and sympathy for his 'crime'.

The pillory stood until 1830 when the last victim, Peter Bosey, was punished for perjury.

SWEENEY TODD, DEMON BARBER OF FLEET STREET

Mention has to be made of Sweeney Todd and his barber's shop, which reputedly stood at No. 186, Fleet Street next to St. Dunstan's Church.

Sweeney Todd first appeared under the title, 'The String of Pearls' in a Victorian Penny Dreadful, Edward Lloyd's *The People's Periodical and Family Library* (21 November 1846 to 20 March 1847), in eighteen weekly parts. James Malcolm Rymer probably wrote the story, although Thomas Peckett Prest has also been credited as the author. Scholars have questioned whether Todd was a real person and the extent to which he is based on an amalgam of different people and different stories. It seems much more likely that the story originated as urban myth, despite attempts to 'prove' that Todd was a real character. There is no doubt that many Londoners in the 1840s and 1850s feared, with good reason, that their sausages and pies were being filled with cheap horsemeat, or worse.

In the original story, set in 1785, Todd was a barber whose shop displayed the famous sign, 'Easy shaving for a penny, as good as you'll find anywhere.' Todd murdered his customers by slitting their throats whilst they sat in the chair then pulled a lever that plunged them into the basement. Once the client had been robbed and murdered the body was put to use by Margaret Lovett, Todd's partner in crime, who chopped them up and made them into meat pies. Mrs. Lovett's pie shop in nearby Bell Yard was connected to the barber's shop by means of an underground passage.

The original title is based on the strange disappearance of a sailor named Lieutenant Thornhill, last seen entering Sweeney Todd's shop bearing a gift of a string of pearls for a girl named Johanna Oakley on behalf of her lover, Mark Ingestrie, who is missing at sea. A seafaring friend, Colonel Jeffery, is alerted to Thornhill's disappearance by his faithful dog, Hector. Johanna, who wants to know what happened to her lover, soon joins Jeffery. Her suspicions of Sweeney Todd lead her to dress up as a boy and work in the barbers shop.

She then discovers the full horror of Todd's activities when the dismembered remains of hundreds of his victims are discovered in the crypt underneath St. Dunstan's church.

Her lover, Mark Ingestrie, who had been imprisoned in the cellars beneath the pie-shop, was working as a cook and escaped via the lift used to bring the pies up from the cellar into the pie-shop. In a dramatic announcement to startled customers he stated: 'Ladies and Gentlemen – I fear that what I am going to say will spoil your appetites . . . Mrs Lovett's pies are made of human flesh!'

The story of Sweeney Todd sees him end his days at the end of a rope in January 1802 outside Newgate Prison before a crowd of thousands.

Sweeny Todd has also been adapted for stage and screen. It appeared as a melodrama in 1847 at Hoxton's Britannia Theatre, and was billed as 'founded on fact'. Various versions of the tale were staples of the British theatre for the rest of the century. The first film version was in 1926, although is now lost. Other film versions appeared in 1928, 1936, 1946, 1970 and 2001. The most recent was the Tim Burton adaptation with Johnny Depp and Helena Bonham Carter in 2007. Sweeney Todd has also been adapted for radio (first in 1947), a ballet (1959 – with the Royal Ballet Company); TV in 1970, 1973, 1998 and with Ray Winstone as Sweeny Todd in 2006; a musical in 1979; as a song in 1956 by Stanley Holloway; a Broadway musical in 2005; and an audio play (2007).

CHAPTER SIX

SHOWS AND ENTERTAINMENT

London teemed with features of the carnivalesque and all its pleasures. The 'world as a stage' analogy can be made with many places of popular pleasures as well as the grotesque. The behaviour of the crowd on execution days was not dissimilar from that in the theatre, alehouse, blood sports or street entertainments. Shows, fairs, festivals and entertainments constituted much of the moving pageant of London from the twelfth century. These events could be robust, sometimes bizarre, anarchic and violent.

The theatre of the crowd was a familiar part of London's history, and the capital teemed with the pleasures of sex, sin, eating, drinking, and bawdy entertainment. Men playing football in the street was a common sight. Itinerant puppeteers, or 'motion men', accompanied jugglers, tumblers, and musicians, who were active in London fairs such as those at Smithfield. Puppet shows found audiences around Holborn and Fleet Street where they were held in high regard during the sixteenth and seventeenth centuries. Animals, freaks, bizarre shows, exotic entertainers, minstrels, fortune-tellers, and itinerant beggars all contributed to this street theatre. Peter Ackroyd compared London to the gargantuan carnival monster, in its monstrous, gigantic, fleshy, and voracious form, growing fat upon its appetite for 'people and for food, for goods and for drink; it consumes and it excretes, maintained within a continual state of greed and desire'.

Fleet Street was not only a major thoroughfare for this flow of entertainment but also a venue for a wide variety of shows and pleasures. Many could be typically boisterous such as the annual burning of the Pope (17 November) during the reign of Charles II (1660-1685). A torchlight parade began in Moorfields and ended at the Middle Temple gatehouse with the burning of an effigy of the Pope. After the reign of James II (1685-1688) the procession was transferred to 5 November. William Hogarth illustrated the scene in *Burning of the Rumps at Temple Bar*, although this depicts the burning of effigies from the Rump Parliament.

Shoe Lane had a notorious cockpit in Pepys's time. It was a round amphitheatre-like building where cockfighting took place. Samuel Pepys records a visit to the cockpit in 1663 where he commented on the 'strange variety of people from Parliamentarian . . . to the poorest prentices, bakers, brewers, butchers, dairymen and what not; and all these fellows one with another cursing and betting'. Shortly after, the Great Fire of 1666 destroyed much of the street.

A curious public were as happy looking at the model giants striking the hours on St. Dunstan's clock as they were at the sight of a legless fourteen-year old child, measuring only eighteen inches, who could be seen at a grocer's in Shoe Lane, at the sign of the Eagle and Child. At the Blue Boar's Head in the 1690s a Polynesian, brought to England by the navigator William Dampier, was exhibited. A handbill described the native as the 'Painted Prince.' In 1702 a model of Amsterdam, thirty feet long by twenty feet wide, which had taken twelve years to make, was exhibited in Bell Yard. At the White Horse, 'where the great elephant was displayed', a huge Lincolnshire ox, nineteen hands high and four yards long was on view. Between the Queen's Head and the Crooked Billet near Fleet Bridge were exhibited daily 'the greatest rarity and novelty that ever was seen in the three kingdoms, two strange, wonderful, and remarkable monstrous creatures – an old female dromedary, seven feet high and ten feet long, lately arrived from Tartary, and her young one'.

The use of taverns for many exhibitions was of no surprise. Throughout the seventeenth and eighteenth centuries, taverns in busy areas such as Fleet Street, Strand, Charing Cross and Westminster were more than happy to take advantage of their space by renting out for the use of exhibitions, which would always be popular with passers-by.

Quacks and charlatans abounded and often took to the streets to promote their miracle cures. Ned Ward tells of a quack who, on seeing a brawl in Fleet Street, was quick to make the most of a ready assembled crowd. He dismounted his horse and pulled out a 'packet of universal hodge-podge', and began to address the crowd:

> Gentlemen, you have that mind to be mindful of preserving a sound mind in a sound body . . . the learned Doctor Honorificabilitudinitaibusque has it, Manus Sanaque in Cobile Sanaquorum, may here at the expense of sixpence, furnish himself with a parcel, which though tis but small, yet containeth mighty things of great use.

He also produced a pill, *Pillula Tondobula,* that 'contained wonderful virtue's which promised to cure 'twenty distempers lurking in the mass of blood'. The man had many more marvels of medicine including an 'excellent plaster' guaranteed to heal wounds, ulcers, pains, and aches, whether they be in the head, bowels or limbs; a sixpenny powder, 'the most powerful medicine ever given in England', to fortify the stomach against all infections. So incredible was the powder that it could burrow into the body as 'rabbits in a warren, come creeping out at both ends, like lice out of a beggar's doublet when he hangs it in the sunshine'.

The mountebank clearly had a way with words and was not short on hyperbole, which was evident in the promotion of his last, but best, medicine in the universe. The 'Orvietan whose virtues are such, it will, equally with the unicorn's horn, expel the rankest poison'. This elixir was to be carried at all times, as it was 'the greatest cordial that the most eminent doctor can prescribe or patient's take'.

Ned Ward despaired that the 'brainless multitude' could show so much eagerness to untie their purses and throw away what little money they had. As for the physician who rode away with his takings, Ward was particularly scathing:

> I can't imagine what can be urged as an excuse for tolerating such rascals to drain the pockets of the poor by preposterous lies, jumbled into a senseless cant . . . a means is needed to dissuade the public from their foolish opinion of these empirical vagabonds and their medicines, which are only prepared from a parcel of perished drugs.

Fleet Street also had its resident quacks. Doctor Johnson's old friend and servant, the quack 'Doctor' Levett, was described as an 'obscure practiser in physick amongst the lower people in the neighbouring Alsatia'. Another quack by the name of Mr. Patence ran a business at Bow Court between 1771 and 1776, and doubled as both doctor and dentist. He announced in the *London Gazette*, with no concession to modesty, that the nobility could attest to the success of his medicines and his cures. His operations, he added, were superior to all other dentists and physicians in the kingdom. He claimed that his 'Universal Medicine treated palsies, gout, rheumatism, piles, cancers of any sort, the King's Evil [scrofula], jaundice, green sickness, hereditary infections, convulsions, consumption, pains in the head, brain, temple, arteries, face, nose, mouth and limbs'. All this came at two prices – three shillings, or ten shillings and sixpence.

In 1710 the *Tatler* reported on the exhibition of a moving picture at the Duke of Marlborough's Head in Fleet Street. William Pinkethman, a popular low comedian who was also a fair booth impresario, introduced this 'new' form of mechanical entertainment to London. The 'moving picture' involved a number of cut-out figures activated by hidden clockwork that made them perform repetitive motions. The following year at the same place, 'the great posture-master of Europe' was said to greatly startle sight-seeing London as

> he extends his body into all deformed shapes; makes his hip and shoulder-bones meet together; lays his head upon the ground, and turns his body round twice or thrice, without stirring his face from the spot; stands upon one leg, and extends the other in a perpendicular line half a yard above his head; and extends his body from a table with his head a foot below his heels, having nothing to balance his body but his feet; with several other postures too tedious to mention.

One of the most well known entertainments on Fleet Street was Mrs. Salmon's waxworks. Mrs. Salmon (1650-1740), who established a waxworks long before Madame Tussaud, was a toymaker and by all accounts something of an eccentric who would wear a white crepe cap with coffin trimmings and sleep in a shroud. She ran a show with her husband from 1693 and moved her collection of waxworks from St Martin-Le-Grand to the Horn tavern on the north side of Fleet Street in 1711. Her collection consisted of historical, mythical, horrific, comical and fantastical personalities and events. An advertisement of Mrs. Salmon's waxwork in the *Tatler* specified, among other attractions,

> the Turkish Seraglio in wax-work, the Fatal Sisters that spin, reel, and cut the thread of man's life, an Old Woman flying from Time, who shakes his head and hour-glass with sorrow at seeing age so unwilling to die. Nothing but life can exceed the motions of the heads, hands, eyes, etc, of these figures.

The German musician Johann Friedrich Armand von Uffenbach (1687-1769) wrote travel journals providing much fascinating information about the period and the places he visited. He was critical of most things English so it was no surprise that he was not pleased with Mrs. Salmon's waxworks. It did not matter to Londoners because they loved it, including Dr. Johnson's friend and companion, James Boswell, who was a regular visitor. People would pay sixpence and enter through the toyshop on the ground floor up to the candle-lit rooms on the first floor. Uffenbach informs us that

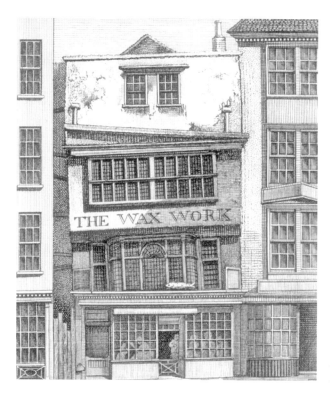

Mrs. Salmon's waxworks in 1793

there were 'six rooms full of all kinds of wax figures, mostly life size and representing ancient tales, especially English ones . . . her work is tolerable, though Frau Braunin in Frankfort makes much more elegant work'. Had he been able to visit later in the century, he would have also seen waxworks of George III and Queen Charlotte, the Prince of Wales, General Wolfe and Dr. Johnson, John Wilkes with a cracked nose, John Wesley conversing with Dick Turpin, shepherds with their lambs and goats, and a man-of-war in wax upon a sea of glass. There was also a figure of the witch Old Mother Shipton who kicked astonished visitors as they left.

In 1795 Mrs. Salmon's waxworks were moved to more spacious apartments at the corner of the Inner Temple Gate, the Palace of Prince Henry. The waxworks were exhibited here until 1816 and included a waxwork of former neighbour 'Sweeney Todd and his famous original chair'.

In the *Spectator* of 5 April 1711, Joseph Addison commented on

> the great Trouble and Inconvenience which Ladies were at, in travelling up and down to the several Shows that are exhibited in different Quarters of the Town. The dancing Monkeys are in one place; the Puppet-Show in another; the Opera in a third; not to mention the Lions.

A lion from Barbary was shown at the Duke of Marlborough's Head. It was billed as so wonderfully 'tame that any person may handle' it. In addition, the exhibition also included a 'noble panther', and a 'noble pelican or vulture' – clearly there was some uncertainty about this creature. The 'neither man nor beast' category was always a crowd puller such as the 'little Black Hairy Pigmy' (a baboon) bred in the deserts of Arabia, which was shown at the White Horse Inn, Fleet Street. Described as two feet high, with a natural ruff of hair about his face, he was said to walk upright and drink a glass of ale or wine.

There were many other exotic entertainments on Fleet Street. *The Manners and Customs of London During the Eighteenth Century* (1810) records for 1718 the juggling exhibition of a fire-eater by the name of De Hightrehight, a native of the valley of Annivi in the Alps, who performed five times per day, at the Duke of Marlborough's Head in Fleet Street:

> [This] tremendous person ate burning coals, chewed flaming brimstone and swallowed it, licked a red-hot poker, placed a red-hot heater on his tongue, kindled coals on his tongue, suffered them to be blown, and broiled meat on them, ate brimstone, bees-wax, sealing wax, and rosin, with a spoon.

Automaton clocks and giants and dwarves, proved to be hugely popular. The clock at the end of Wine Office Court had three statues, which on a given command variously poured out red or white wine, a grocer shut up his shop and the figure of a black man struck a bell.

Real giants, as opposed to model ones, included a seven-foot Essex woman, named Gordon, an Italian giantess who was even taller and Edward Bamford, seven feet four inches tall who was buried in St. Dunstan's churchyard. A fee of £200 was offered for his body to be used for dissection. Amongst the dwarf exhibits was a German named Buckinger who was only twenty-nine inches high and, although he had no legs or hands, he could write, thread a needle, shuffle a pack of cards and play skittles; the so-called Black Prince and his wife both stood at three feet high, and a Turkish horse two feet high was exhibited with them. By 1822, sensitivities were clearly changing when the Lord Chamberlain put a stop to the exhibition of a mermaid.

Rackstraw's Museum of Anatomy and Natural Curiosities, which closed in the early nineteenth century, was on Fleet Street between Temple Bar and Chancery Lane. He died in 1772 and Richard Altick in his book *The Shows of London* (1978) informs us that his 'museum' came to be an eclectic mix of waxworks, which included a whale skeleton, a miscellany of birds, shells, skull, skeletons, fossils, stuffed crocodiles, the death masks of Oliver Cromwell and Isaac Newton and a mummy said to be Pharaoh's daughter.

Edward Donovan's Collection of Natural History proved to be less successful whilst Powell's Puppet Show enlivened the precincts. In 1745 at the junction of Fleet Street and Shoe Lane, an exhibition took place that involved a tableau with 1000 miniature figures displaying various scenes from Samuel Richardson's novel *Pamela*.

The presence of a black community in London was evident from a newspaper report in 1764 that described how fifty-seven black men and women ate, drank, and entertained themselves with dancing and music – from violins, French horns and other instruments – until four in the morning at a public-house in Fleet Street. No white people were allowed to be present and all the performers were black. John Diprose, in his *Some account of the parish of Saint Clement Danes* (1868-76), tells of a particular character known as Charles M'Ghee or 'Brutus Billy', whose father had died in Jamaica at the age of 108. M'Ghee swept a crossing on Fleet Street for many years. At night, after he had finished work, he carried round a basket of nuts and fruit to places of public entertainment, so that in time he amassed a considerable amount of money. He died in Chapel Court in 1854, in his eighty-seventh year.

THEATRES

Fleet Street has not had a strong tradition of theatres. The first theatre in Whitefriars appears to have been built in the hall of the old White Friars Monastery in the late sixteenth century. It had become disreputable by 1609, and ruinous in 1619, when 'the rain made its way in'. Theatres fell victim to Puritan piety and after 1580 such godly people saw playhouses and dicing-houses as traps for the young and gullible. Nonetheless many theatres found homes outside of the City. Early theatres such as the Whitefriars and the Bell Savage on Ludgate Hill were, like many in the sixteenth and early seventeenth century, makeshift structures rather than an indoor theatre. They were made of temporary scaffolds erected at inn-yards, and the theatre at Whitefriars was more likely to have been in the old refectory of the Carmelite friars or at some inn-yard.

Further Puritan zeal during the Civil War curtailed plays, although some were performed illegally at Salisbury Court Theatre until soldiers destroyed it in 1649. After the Restoration, it was restored by William Beeston and was one of the first theatres to re-open. It was variously called the 'Salisbury Court,' 'Davenant's,' or 'Duke's ' Theatre'. It was built near the south east end of Salisbury Court with a fine stone frontage, a flight of steps to the river, and an imposing façade towards the north.

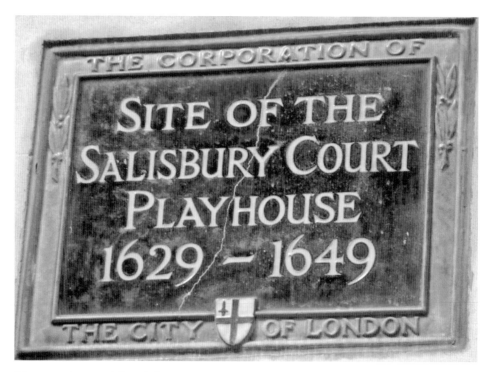

Plaque on the site of the Salisbury Court Theatre

South façade of the Dorset Garden Theatre from an engraving by William Dolle first published in the libretto of The Empress of Morocco, *1673*

Amphitheatra *file et Spectacula Barbara Cesar:*
Non eveunt Nudi non Aper, Ursa, Leo.
Nos Miles colimus Mis'us lentivi Amorq3
Bella, eym nostro est Onrobi Marte Venus,
Quæfq3 fecerat olim Thalamo cepiffe Theatro
Ludentes una cernat Apolla Oeos.

THE DUKE'S THEATRE.
Dorset Garden.

In February 1661, Samuel Pepys paid a visit to the Whitefriars to see *The Mad Lover* and noted that it was 'the first time I ever saw it acted, which I liked pretty well'. Three days later he was less pleased, adding that he did not like the seats and 'went out again'. Not deterred he went back on 2 March and found 'the house as full as could be', for a production of *The Queene's Maske*. The production of *Tis Pity She's a Whore* on 9 September was not to his taste, although typical of him he found the female audience more appealing than the play: 'It was my fortune to sit by a most pretty and most ingenious lady, which pleased me very much.' Five years later the theatre was destroyed in the Great Fire, and a plaque marks the site of the theatre. Theatre promoter John Downes wrote in his *Roscius Anglicanus* (1708) that 'on the 9th day of November 1671, they opened their new theatre . . . which continued acting three days together, with a full audience each day'.

After the Restoration a new playhouse was built, the Dorset Garden Theatre, which stood slightly south of the Salisbury Court Theatre by the Thames. It was considered to be the finest playhouse of its day with approaches to it by land and water. The theatre was renowned for its magnificent staging. For the production of *The Lancashire Witches* in 1681 there were several 'flying machines for the witches, and other diverting contrivances.' Also in the 1680s, the production of the *Empress of Morocco* had splendid scenery, prisons, palaces, combats of long duration, a dancing tree, a rainbow, a shower of hail, an executed criminal, and hell itself opening upon the stage.

As the fashion for theatre in London moved west so the actors and company moved also. Unfortunately, after fifteen years, the early reputation of the Dorset Garden Theatre was gone and it began to provide more base entertainment such as jugglers, wild beats trainers and strong men. In 1689 it was renamed the Queen's Theatre. An advertisement in *The Post Boy*, 8 December 1699, gives an idea of the quality of the acts:

> The famous Kentishmen, Wm And Rich Joy design to show the town before they leave it, trials of strength . . . The lifting of a weight of two thousand two hundred pounds. His holding an extraordinary large cart horse and breaking a rope which will bear three thousand five hundred pounds weight.

Blackfriars Theatre at the western end of Fleet Street was described in 1618 as a venue where such a great mass of people and coaches descend that

> [the] streets could not contain them, they clogged up Ludgate Hill . . . inhabitants were unable to get to their houses, or ring in their provisions . . . Quarrels and effusion of blood had followed, and other dangers might be occasioned by the broils, plots and practices of such an unruly multitude.

THE PRESS

Early Printers and Booksellers

From a very early stage, Fleet Street was the accepted home of those who gained a living by the production of books, just as it was, to a certain extent, the home of those engaged in their making. Booksellers hawked their wares like peddlers, whereas the stationer was someone who kept a shop or stall in a stationary place, and there was an abundance of both of these in the area. Stationers often sold the materials that went towards the making of books, as well as the completed article. It was not uncommon for book selling and publishing to be carried out together. This was especially the case when the printer published and sold books, as did Caxton at Westminster and Wynkyn de Worde in Fleet Street in the early sixteenth century. Although Fleet Street's most famous association is with the press, this had to wait until later.

We have already mentioned how William Caxton's apprentice, Wynken de Worde, set up a printing press in Fleet Street in 1498. This was at the sign of the *Sun* next to St. Bride's Church. It was an appropriate location, given Fleet Street's importance as a major thoroughfare between the commercial centre of the City of London and the Court and Abbey at Westminster. In addition, Fleet Street had already established itself as first a monastic location, and a legal one. Given such a concentration of literary professions, there would inevitably be a demand for scriveners to write out copies of religious and legal documents.

Plaque to Wynken de Worde

Wynken's output had been prodigious. He produced over 700 publications in a period of forty years. It was de Worde who began the commercialization of the production of printed books in England. He laid the foundations for commercial publishing by popularising a great variety of books: children's books, short histories, poetry, romances, instructions for pilgrims, marriage, household practice, and animal husbandry. Wynken de Worde, who was buried in St. Bride's Churchyard in 1534, can rightly claim the title of 'Father of Fleet Street' with regard to the tradition of publishing.

De Worde and those who came after him were not only printers but also booksellers, selling their products from the premises where they had their presses. Fleet Street provided the ideal location as a busy area with many customers, both resident and passers-by.

Richard Pynson, Henry VII's printer, followed De Worde into Fleet Street at the sign of St George at Chancery Lane corner. By the mid-sixteenth century, Fleet Street contained many bookshops. At the sign of the Falcon, near St. Dunstan's Church, William Griffith printed books that he sold at his second shop above the Conduit in Fleet Street. At the George, William Powell published religious books. Richard Tottell stayed at the Hand and Star, just within Temple Bar, where he sent scores of books to distinguished men. Queen Elizabeth I, in 1577, granted the privilege of printing to 'all kinds of Law books'. Other printers came to the area such as Julian Notary, John Wayland, John Butler, and Robert Copland who all paved the way for the long tradition of publishing in Fleet Street. Typical of an industry that had been imported, many printers were migrants such as De Worde and Pynson. Not surprisingly, descendents of Huguenot's were prominent among London printers well into the nineteenth century.

By the seventeenth century many booksellers were based around St. Dunstan's Churchyard, including Thomas Marsh who issued *Stow's Chronicles*; J. Smethwicke who sold Shakespeare's *Hamlet, Love's Labour Lost, Romeo and Juliet, Taming of the Shrew*, in addition to works by other authors; Richard Marriot who sold Isaac Walton's *Complete Angler*, for 1s 6d; and Abel Roper, publisher of the *Post Boy* newspaper.

Edmund Curll produced his publications from the sign of the Dial and Bible, against St. Dunstan's Church. Curll's career was colourful to say the least. The occasion on which he was fined for selling indecent literature and placed in the pillory at Charing Cross was only one of many colourful incidents. Trouble followed Curll (1675-1747) largely because he courted it, and his bookselling activities are full of misdemeanours including breaches of privileges, offences against taste, and offences against morals. *Mist's Weekly Journal* for 5 April 1718 describes Curll as a 'contemptible wretch in a thousand ways; he is odious in his person, scandalous in his fame: more beastly, insufferable books have been published by this one offender than in thirty years before by all the nation'.

Curll had few scruples about how he made his money and would have fitted in quite comfortably in the contemporary world of tabloid journalism. He cashed in on scandals, published pornography, offered patent medicine, and exploited all publicity, good or bad. By managing a small empire of printing houses, he was well placed to promote his business. He was notorious for commissioning hack-written biographies of famous people as soon as they died, and for publishing them without regard for inaccuracies and inventions. When he could not get contributions from people for his biographies, he would hire an author to invent material. His sole objective was to be the first into the shops with a posthumous biography. Inaccuracy mattered little.

Perhaps his main claim to fame, or infamy, was his indecent publications. He was so well known for these that the term 'Curlism' was coined as a synonym for indecent literature. In 1723, he published *A Treatise of the Use of Flogging in Venereal Affairs*, and in 1724 he published *The Nun in her Smock*, a pornographic title, which argued that it is the Church, and not Christ, that forbids sexual exploration. Shortly after the publication he was arrested but the courts determined that there was no actual obscenity law, so they prosecuted him for libel. Ever the one to cash in on an opportunity, negative or positive, Curll published an apology and promised to quit publishing, but the apology was an advert for two new titles. Curll and his son Henry spent fourteen months in prison for publishing state secrets from the reign of Queen Anne, as well as being fined and sentenced to an hour in the pillory. Curll published a broadsheet by way of explanation for his actions. It worked and the crowd cheered Curll and carried him away on their shoulders.

Other booksellers along Fleet Street were John Starkey, of the Mitre, and Thomas Dring, of the George, near Clifford's Inn. An early rivalry between two Fleet Street booksellers, Robert Redman and Richard Pynson, arose when Redman stole Pynson's material. Pynson called Redman the 'rudest out of a thousand men . . . this scoundrel did profess himself a Bookseller.'

Thomas Berthelet, printer to the King, was evidently a man of importance. He employed other printers to produce the works he published, notably Tyndale's Bible, which was printed for him by Redman in 1540. In fact the title pages of seventeenth-century books reveal the names of many publishers and printers connected with Fleet Street.

The Civil War had stimulated a thirst for regular newssheets that carried information about events as well as propaganda. Between 1640 and the Restoration, around 30,000 'news letters' and 'news papers' were printed. Although a range of publications such as broadsheets, pamphlets and ballads had been produced, the first 'newspapers' were slow to evolve. Following the Restoration in 1660, a number of publications emerged including the *London Gazette* (first published on 16 November 1665 as the *Oxford Gazette*), the first official journal on record, and the newspaper of the Crown. However, publication in general was controlled under the Licensing Act of 1662. When this control was abolished in 1694, many new titles flourished, and in 1712 there were about twenty single-leaf papers.

The Eighteenth Century

The eighteenth century saw a proliferation of newspapers. It was an exciting time for publishing when so much was written of permanent value, as well as merely ephemeral importance. In 1702 Elizabeth Mallett launched the first successful and regular English daily newspaper, the *Daily Courant*. It was based next to the King's Arms tavern where Mallett claimed that she intended to publish only foreign news, and declared she had established her paper to 'spare the public at least half the impertinences which the ordinary papers contain'. After nine issues, Samuel Buckley took over the *Courant* in 1705 and moved it to premises in the area of Little Britain in Smithfield. In 1735 the *Daily Courant* was merged with the *Daily Gazetteer*.

With the emergence of newspapers there was also a rise of the journalist, and Grub Street became associated with this practice. Grub Street was a real street near Moorgate,

Plaque to the Daily Courant

and it was here that the foundations of Fleet Street and the modern newspaper were laid. Samuel Johnson's *Dictionary* defines Grub Street as being 'originally the name of a street . . . much inhabited by writers of small histories, dictionaries, and temporary poems, whence any mean production is called grubstreet.'

In 1830, the street's name was changed to Milton Street after a local builder. Grub Street was an area of poverty, vice, disreputable tenements, brothels and alleys. It was also a place associated with writers and publishers. However, as Bob Clarke says in *From Grub Street to Fleet Street* (2004), there is little evidence to support the view that it 'played host to a colony of impoverished writers'. There were many destitute writers who lived around Grub Street and as such, it became synonymous with the hack writer – a writer for hire – and by association the 'lower reaches of literature and journalism'.

The free licence on publications had allowed many cheap papers to prosper and proliferate. However, a great number of the sensationalist publications ended when the first penny newspaper stamp was imposed in 1712. Swift sarcastically announced the demise of these papers when he commented, 'all Grub Street is dead and gone . . . No more ghosts or murders now for love or money'. Sensationalist material would prove more enduring than Swift's lament. The press continued to offer a regular diet of 'shocking and sensational news' down to present times. Oliver Goldsmith, writing half a century after Swift, in the *Public Ledger,* cynically summed up the Grub Street tradition, as well as pre-empting the worse type of Fleet Street hack:

> You must not imagine that they who compile these papers have any actual knowledge of the politics or government of the State; they only collect their materials from the oracle of some coffee-house, which oracle has himself gathered them the night before from a beau at a gaming table, who has pillaged his knowledge from a great man's porter, who has had information from the great man's gentleman, who has invented the whole story for his own amusement the night preceding.

The works of the great figures in English literature were published and sold in Fleet Street. Indeed some of the authors actually lived there. In Gough Square, Dr. Johnson compiled much of his *Dictionary* between 1748 and 1758. In Salisbury Court, Samuel Richardson, author of the first English novel, *Pamela* (and the better-known *Clarissa*) lived, printed, published, and wrote his books; Oliver Goldsmith passed the closing years of his life in Brick Court off Middle Temple Lane; Samuel Pepys was born in Salisbury Court; Essayist Charles Lamb (1775-1834) lived variously in Chancery Lane, Mitre Court and close to Inner Temple; bookseller Bernard Lintot issued Alexander Pope's *Homer* at Middle Temple Gate; and Benjamin Motte published Swift's *Gulliver's Travels,* for which he had grudgingly given only £200. Of all the second-hand booksellers of the later part of the eighteenth century the most considerable stock was that of Benjamin White. His shop was at the sign of Horace's Head in Fleet Street, and his bulky catalogues often included over 10,000 volumes.

By the early nineteenth century there were fifty-two London papers and over 100 other titles. Although book selling and production began to find homes elsewhere, Fleet Street maintained its reputation for producing well-known publications such as the *Political Register* edited by William Cobbett who lived on the north side of Fleet Street and the *John Bull* newspaper which began in 1820 in Johnson's Court. There was also the notable name of John Murray, one of Britain's most distinguished literary publishers,

Fleet Street in the 1860s. A painting by Ernest George (1839-1922)

who started out at the Falcon. This was the beginning of a remarkable and prosperous career culminating in the great publishing house of Murray. From its foundation in 1768, the firm published authors such as Byron, Darwin and Jane Austen.

The satirical magazine *Punch* was born at No. 3 Crane Court and the first edition was published on 17 July 1841. Its founders, wood engraver Ebenezer Landells and writer Henry Mayhew, got the idea for the magazine from a satirical French paper, *Charivari* which they used in the subtitle of *Punch* – 'The London Charivari'. In its early years, it was radical and published poems such as Thomas Hood's 'Song of the Shirt', an attack against sweated labour. By the 1860s the magazine became less inclined to attack the Establishment or support the underdog. A succession of superb artists on *Punch* left a memorable picture of Victorian England. By the late twentieth century circulation declined and it was eventually closed in 1992, but relaunched in 1996 by Harrods proprietor, Mohamed Al Fayed. Sadly it was not to last and closed again in 2002, leaving a legacy of some of the finest humour and wit in publishing history.

Before the arrival of large circulating national newspapers there was an array of local papers, provincial journals, satirical magazines, scientific, sporting, and medical news-sheets. The *Gentleman's Magazine* was partly printed in Red Lion Court from 1779 to 1781 and Charles Knight's very popular *Penny Magazine*, was inaugurated in Fleet Street in 1832. Companies such as Parkins of Salisbury Square and Read of Whitefriars issued halfpenny newssheets and other enterprising eighteenth century publications three times a week. It was no coincidence that the mix of Grub Street hacks, the King's printer, and radicals such as Hardy and Carlile were together in this cultural melting pot of a printing tradition, whose roots had been planted by De Worde and the early presses.

However, by the nineteenth century Fleet Street could not rival the preceding century in the production books. Nonetheless there were still companies involved in diverse kinds of publications such as Mr. Cruchley's, Mapseller and Globe Manufacturer. Despite the decline in book production, Fleet Street would establish itself as the place where national newspapers were published and it is with this industry that it would become synonymous.

The Newspaper Industry

London's first daily newspaper, the *Daily Courant*, was printed at the east end of Fleet Street whilst the first evening newspaper, the *Star*, was published at Temple Bar. The *Star*, founded by Peter Stuart, survived until 1831 when it was incorporated with the *Albion*. Although these were important newspaper milestones for Fleet Street, newspaper production in the eighteenth century was based very much in the Strand and the area west of Paternoster Row.

Fleet Street's connection with the newspaper industry was very much a nineteenth century product. However, even by the beginning of the nineteenth century, not a single one of London's daily papers (apart from the evening *Star*) was published in Fleet Street. The *Morning Advertiser*, founded in 1794, only migrated to Fleet Street in 1825. Fleet Street was well placed to accommodate the shift of news production from the Strand. Fleet Street had the advantages of being at the heart of the printing industry, and it was closer to City intelligence. The seeds were thus sown for the rapid growth of purpose-built newspaper offices.

There was a spectacular growth in print particularly from the 1820s. The importance of the interplay between social, economic and technological developments in the period between 1830 and 1890 that contributed to the expansion of the written word was huge. One example of a company that profited from these changes was W. H. Smith, based in nearby Strand. They were quick to capture and exploit the provision of news supply to the cities by switching from the use of stagecoaches to railways, which in turn accounted for the proliferation of railway bookstalls. Early newspapers had suffered from a combination of being too brief, printed on poor quality paper and, before the coming of the railways, having limited circulation.

By the late nineteenth century huge changes made possible the transition from small-scale circulation to mass circulation. These changes included developments in transport, the removal of taxation on papers, as well as taxes on advertisements. With the introduction of the Education Act in 1870 there was a growth in literacy, and a new reading public. Printing techniques saw a shift towards rotary presses by 1870, fed by great rolls of paper. With the development of the chemical treatment of wood pulp as a means of producing the raw material for newsprint, the transition was complete.

The telephone, and especially the telegraph, revolutionised news production and distribution, which flowed in abundance from London. In 1868, the Press Association moved to offices in Wine Office Court, and made use of telegraphic news production for provincial papers to London. Fleet Street became the hub of news and activity, so it was not surprising that papers moved there. W. E. Henley's *Scottish Observer* moved from Edinburgh to London in 1892, as did the *Clarion*, a socialist paper founded in Manchester in 1891.

It was also by the late nineteenth century that most of the well-known national newspapers were based on or around Fleet Street. The majority of papers were not on the actual street at all. The *Times* was in Blackfriars; the *Daily Mail* and *News Chronicle* in Tudor and Bouverie Streets and the *Daily Mirror* in Fetter Lane.

In December 1820 the office of the weekly *John Bull* magazine was established at 11 Johnson's Court, off Fleet Street. Its success, which was immediate, was built on being scurrilous and abusive. A notorious Tory newspaper edited by Theodore Hook, it was established to counteract the popular enthusiasm for Queen Caroline, wife of King George IV, and her Whig supporters. It was said that Hook's reckless humour was never displayed to so much advantage as in 'this scurrilous, scandalous, but irresistibly facetious, and for a time exceedingly potent journal'. Even at the high price of seven pence it was selling 12,000 copies by its twelfth number.

Businessmen followed, such as Edward Lloyd who provided a mass market for cheap literature. With his office based near Fleet Street he began publishing popular weeklies from the early 1840s and became associated with the 'Penny Dreadfuls' or the Salisbury Square fictions.

It was Colonel Arthur Burroughes Sleigh who started the *Daily Telegraph* in 1855 as a single sheet costing twopence. The *Daily Telegraph* originally started on the Strand, then moved to Fleet Street in 1862 where it remained until it vacated its building in 1987. Sleigh founded the paper with the object of carrying out a vendetta against the Duke of Cambridge, but this proved to be a financial disaster for Sleigh. He had to sell the paper to Joseph Moses Levy who was already the chief proprietor of the *Sunday Times* (it became known as the *Sunday Times* in 1822 but had no relationship with the *Times)*. Levy turned the paper around by reducing the cost to a penny, keeping advertising rates low and using the slogan 'the largest, best, and cheapest newspaper in the world'. Circulation increased to 141,000 copies within six years and it was outselling the *Times*.

However by the 1920s sales declined. The paper was antiquated and in need of re-equipping. It had an eighty-three-year-old editor running it with no news editor or news desk and a handful of staff, mainly old men, wearing green baize aprons. At night, a night editor produced the paper with five staff that worked in what resembled a library with horsehair sofas. In 1927 the paper was taken over by two brothers from Wales, William and Gomer Berry (later Lord Camrose and Lord Kemsley). The Berry brothers did what Levy had once done and halved the price of the paper, which in turn saw circulation rise to half a million.

William Berry, Lord Camrose, died in 1954 and his son, Michael Berry (Lord Hartwell) succeeded him. In doing so he maintained a rigid in-house style that tended, at times, to appear pompous. He said he was always shocked when other people ran their newspapers like biscuit factories, just to make money. His objective was to make the *Telegraph* an institution which was respected and admired, and 'which would leave the world the poorer if it were not there. It sounds awfully boring, but I regarded it as my life's work.' In 1960 *The Sunday Telegraph* was launched, but by the 1980s the Berry brothers could not afford to modernise and they sold the paper

THE
FIRST NUMBER
OF
THE SUNDAY TIMES
WAS EDITED AT
4 SALISBURY COURT
BY
HENRY WHITE
OCTOBER 20
1822

Left: *Plaque to the* Sunday Times *on Salisbury Court*

Opposite: Daily Telegraph *building on Fleet Street*

to Conrad Black in 1985. Shortly after this, the *Telegraph* moved from its long time home in Fleet Street to the Isle of Dogs.

The former Elcock and Sutcliffe *Daily Telegraph* building (1928-31), now owned by Goldman Sachs Bank, stands at 135-41, Fleet Street. The street façade has something of the Selfridge's look about it, with a screen of giant columns in a Graeco-Egyptian fashion. Fleet Street has other examples of narrow fronted office buildings, which eventually replaced the wooden framed and brick houses during the nineteenth century. A particular example is at 133 Fleet Street, next door to the Daily Telegraph building. This is Mersey House (1904-6), built to the design of an unknown architect to house the London offices of the *Liverpool Daily Post*.

One of the most spectacular of popular journalists and newspaper publishers in the history of the British press was Alfred Harmsworth (1865-1922), who later became Lord Northcliffe. Described by some as bad, mad, and dangerous to know, he founded his print dynasty in 1888 as a free-lance contributor to popular periodicals. Harmsworth had made his money in the 1890s with publications such as the *Comic Cuts, Illustrated Chips* and *Answers*. In 1894 he bought the *London Evening News,* which launched his career in newspaper publishing. Other publications were gradually acquired that formed the basis for what became the world's largest periodical combine, the Amalgamated Press. With his brother Harold (later Viscount Rothermere) as his financial administrator, circulation of his papers increased. Northcliffe initiated popular features such as woman's columns, serials, and social gossip in the papers that he founded such as the *Daily Mail* in 1896 and the *Daily Mirror* in 1903. He went on to gain control of the then struggling *Times* in 1908, helping to get it back on its feet with changes in editorial policy. It was through his newspaper campaigns during the First World War, notably those concerning faulty munitions, national conscription, and food rationing, that Northcliffe was influential in determining certain aspects of the war. His support of Lloyd George in 1916 was instrumental in bringing about the downfall of the Asquith government.

The *Daily Mail* was Britain's first large popular newspaper. It was based at Carmelite House at the junction with Tallis Street. Having had success with the *Evening News*, Harmsworth wanted to launch a daily paper. On 4 May 1896 the *Daily Mail* hit the streets at halfpence a copy – half that of other papers. The front page was full of small advertisements and a campaign to stop men with red flags walking in front of motorcars. The *Daily Mail* marked the commencement of a new epoch in modern journalism, just as the *Telegraph* had done in 1855. From the beginning, the *Mail* set out to entertain its readers with human-interest stories, serials, features and competitions. Harmsworth said when he took this gamble that it could mean 'bankruptcy or Berkeley Square'. It turned out to be Berkeley Square, with initial circulation figures of 400,000 rising eventually to one million. The *Mail's* enterprise and efficiency in the Boer War, which occurred a year after its foundation, helped to raise the circulation to that unprecedented figure. Harmsworth declared 'we have struck a gold mine' and its famous taglines included 'the busy man's daily journal' and the 'penny newspaper for one halfpenny'. Less kindly, but more famously, Prime Minister Robert Cecil, Lord Salisbury, said it was 'written by office boys for office boys'.

In 1906 the paper offered £1,000 for the first flight across the English Channel, and £10,000 for the first flight from London to Manchester. In 1908 the first *Daily Mail* Ideal Home Exhibition was held at London's Olympia exhibition centre, and two years later the *Mail* sponsored the first Channel crossing by an airship and exhibited it around Britain to underline to people, and the Government, the military threat posed by Germany.

When Alfred died in 1924, his brother Harold took over the paper and in the following years it was not without controversy. The faked 'Zinoviev Letter' in 1924 suggested that the British Communist Party was planning a violent revolution and the Labour Party were being pressured into a pact with the Soviet Union. In the 1930s Rothermere's support for the British Union of Fascists was reflected in the papers headline, 'Hurrah for the Blackshirts'. On 1 October 1938, Rothermere sent Hitler a telegram in support of Germany's invasion of the Sudetenland, expressing the hope that 'Adolf the Great' would become a popular figure in Britain. The paper moved to Northcliffe House at the northwest junction of Tudor Street in 1927 where it remained until 1989.

By the 1970s the *Daily Mail* was transformed by its editor Sir David English. Its sales soared dramatically and it also moved from broadsheet to compact format, and in 1982, a Sunday title, the *Mail on Sunday* was launched.

Another popular daily newspaper, the *Daily Mirror,* was founded by Alfred Harmsworth in 1903 and was located near to the junction with Tudor Street until 1905. He launched the *Mirror* as the 'first newspaper for gentlewomen' with copies of the first edition containing the gift of a free mirror. Heralded with tremendous advertising, the first issue sold as a novelty but then the sales steadily declined. It was the first big failure that Harmsworth had made. The paper was re-launched as the *Illustrated Daily Mirror* in 1904, and the following year the paper moved to new premises at nearby Whitefriars Street, where it stayed until 1920. By 1914, when Alfred Harmsworth sold the paper to his younger brother Harold, it had a circulation of over one million.

Opposite: *Bust of Lord Northcliffe designed by Sir Edward Lutyens. It stands outside St. Dunstan-in-the-West Church, Fleet Street*

Between 1920 and 1961 the *Daily Mirror* was located on Fetter Lane. Sales began to decline by the late 1920s, until Harry Bartholomew took over as managing editor. From then on significant changes took place in content, production, and political support for the Labour Party. In 1961 the *Mirror* moved to Holborn Circus and was run by Cecil Harmsworth King, nephew of the founder. King was sacked by the board in 1968 for his call for a new Labour Prime Minister, and was replaced by Hugh Cudlipp who continued until his retirement in 1974. Despite its attempts to give serious news coverage as well as more frivolous items, the *Mirror* was in competition with the *Sun*, which was giving increasing attention to lightweight celebrity features. In 1991, as with many of the national papers based in Fleet Street, the *Mirror* moved east to the Isle of Dogs.

The most successful newspaper in terms of circulation was the *Daily Express*, which was based in Shoe Lane when it was established in 1900. Founded by Arthur Pearson, it struggled financially until Conservative MP William Maxwell Aitken (1879-1964), the first Lord Beaverbrook, bailed it out. Beaverbrook acquired the paper outright in 1916 and used it as a critical vehicle against the coalition government of Prime Minister Herbert Asquith. When Lloyd George became Prime Minister in 1916, Aitkin's support was rewarded when he was made Lord Beaverbrook. Beaverbrook became one of the most powerful newspaper magnates in the world, even forming his own political party in 1930, the United Empire Party. He had an unswerving belief in the British Empire, and gained the reputation of being a fearless political fixer, reflected in the fact that he was one of only three men to serve in the cabinet in both wars. In 1910 he had moved to London from Canada with an already acquired fortune.

In 1933 the *Express* moved to 121-128 Fleet Street, a building that was one of the most prominent examples of art deco architecture in London. The architects were Ellis and Clarke with Sir Owen Williams. Robert Atkinson designed the interiors, and the lobby includes plaster reliefs of industry by Eric Aumonier, lots of silver and gilt including a silvered pendant lamp, as well as an oval staircase. The façade is covered with black Vitrolite and clear glass, with chromium strips. It was described on its opening as 'Britain's most modern building for Britain's most modern newspaper'. Beaverbrook celebrated the completion of the building by launching a sales boost that involved distributing 10,000 pairs of silk stockings to registered readers. With sales of two million copies per day, the highest of any national newspaper in the world, he could afford such ambitious promotions. By 1960 sales had reached the astonishing figure of 4,300,000, making it the largest-ever selling British daily newspaper.

At the time of Beaverbrook's death in 1964, the circulation of the *Express* was at its highest. His son, Max Aitken, could not sustain the success of the newspaper and it was sold in 1977 to Victor Matthews' Trafalgar House Company. Despite a succession of owners and editors, the paper continued to decline. The *Express* was the last national newspaper to leave Fleet Street in 1989. It decamped from its art-deco masterpiece, known as the Black Lubyanka, to a pale imitation just over the river by Blackfriars Bridge. Evelyn Waugh's novel, *Scoop* (1938), is based in no small part around Beaverbrook's empire.

A notable location for a number of newspaper offices, such as the *Daily Mirror*, *News of the World*, *Sun*, *Punch*, *News Chronicle* and the *Daily News*, was Bouverie Street,

Opposite: *The Art Deco style of the* Daily Express *building on Fleet Street*

built in 1799 and named after the landlords, the Pleydell-Bouveries, Earls of Radnor (as is one of the tributaries off this street – Pleydell Street). A notable historical feature of the street is that it was the first in the Fleet Street area to have a print works, which was built for James Moyes in 1824.

One of the papers based there was the *News of the World,* which has been the most financially successful Sunday British newspaper, with sales reaching eight million. The newspaper was first published on 1 October 1843, by John Browne Bell. Priced at just three pence, it was the cheapest newspaper of its time, and was aimed directly at the increasingly literate working class. It quickly established itself as a purveyor of titillation, shock, and criminal news, with its motto, 'All human life is there'. It was based at 30-32 Bouverie Street between 1892 and 1986, on the top of the remains of the Carmelite crypt. Despite being dismissed as a 'scandal sheet' it soon established itself as the most widely read Sunday paper. Its success was down to Sir Emsley Carr, who was editor between 1891 and 1941. Carr, who was knighted in 1918, was a shrewd, self-made Yorkshireman who, in a piece of brilliant understatement said, 'we do not cater for the intelligentsia alone'.

The *News of the World* went up for sale in the 1960s. In 1969 Rupert Murdoch, the Australian media magnate, beat off a rival £34 million offer from Robert Maxwell's Pergamon Press to become the new managing director of his first Fleet Street newspaper. He continued to maintain the paper's coverage of sensation, sex, shock and 'world exclusives'. After his successful acquisition Murdoch announced that, 'anyone interested in journalism and mass newspapers realises that Fleet Street is the heart of it all. To be in Fleet Street is to be at the heart.' As with all his other papers, Murdoch moved the *News of the World* to Wapping in 1986.

Whilst the *News of the World* was the largest selling Sunday newspaper, the *Sun* emerged as Britain's biggest selling daily paper, although never reaching the circulation figures reached by the *Express.* Based at 30 Bouverie Street, it grew out of the demise of the Labour-supporting *Daily Herald,* which closed in 1964. The *Sun* initially struggled, until Rupert Murdoch took it over in 1969. Similar to the *News of the World* it focused on a mix of sex, scandal, jingoism, celebrity, sport, lightweight news, sensational headlines, and its famous page three pin-up. Although the Bouverie Street offices were in desperate need of modernizing, Murdoch resolved the problem by moving in 1986, amid a great deal of controversy, to Wapping.

One of the oldest daily newspapers, *The Times,* was located east of Fleet Street, at Printing House Square, west of St. Andrew's Square, between 1785 and 1974. Founded by John Walter on 1 January 1785 as *The Daily Universal Register,* it changed its name to *The Times* in January 1788. In 1872 John Walter III, the founder's grandson, designed new premises that incorporated a large part on the Queen Victoria Street frontage. *The Times* was the first newspaper to send foreign correspondents to cover particular conflicts. Most notably these included William Howard Russell who covered the Crimean War (1853-56), and later Soviet double agent Kim Philby who served as a correspondent during the Spanish Civil War in the 1930s.

By the end of the nineteenth century the newspaper was struggling financially, until Alfred Harmsworth stepped in and bought the title for £320,000 in 1908. This proved controversial given Harmsworth's association with popular papers, and was summed up in snooty comments such as those of Lloyd George, who said it had become 'a threepenny edition of the *Daily Mail'*. Northcliffe re-equipped its outdated printing plant, reduced the newspaper's price to twopence, and appointed a new editor, Geoffrey Dawson. Jacob Astor took it over in 1922 and it remained with the Astor family until 1967, when it was sold to Canadian publishing magnate Roy Thompson. Notably, in May 1966 it broke with the tradition of featuring advertisements on the front page and started printing news on the front for the first time. In 1974, *The Times* moved to Gray's Inn Road and then to Wapping in 1986.

Britain's oldest Sunday newspaper, the *Observer,* founded in 1791 by W. S. Bourne, was a late arrival to the Fleet Street area when it was located at a site near *The Times'* office in 1969. Suffering significant losses during the 1970s, it was taken over by the Atlantic Richfield Corporation who appointed Donald Trelford as editor. By 1981 it was again bought out, this time by Lonrho, a company that Prime Minister Edward Heath had described once as the 'ugly face of capitalism'. It moved from the Fleet Street area in 1988.

The printing industry brought with it the leading printers, compositors, engravers, and lithographers. With such high literacy rates among this aristocracy of labour it was no surprise that unions followed. By the mid-nineteenth century there were an estimated 300 readers or correctors of the press in London – around half of them working only part time for meagre pay. In 1854 one such reader Henry Vernon, at Bradbury and Evans, which published *Punch* magazine, and his colleague William Richards, invited 150 readers in London to a meeting at which an association was formed to protect their interests. In September 1854, the first meeting took place at the Falcon tavern, Fetter Lane, where it was agreed to form a London Association of Correctors of the Press. The association later relocated first to the Mitre, then to other venues. Years later the association demanded a 10% wage rise, and backed up its claim with a public meeting at which the author Charles Dickens was persuaded to take the chair.

During the First World War, the association affiliated to the TUC. From the 1930s the fortunes of the association rose and fell with those of the Fleet Street print unions, and in 1965 it transferred its engagements to the National Graphical Association (NGA) – the direct descendent of the London Society of Compositors. Other mergers followed, notably with the Society of Graphical and Allied Trades representing the less skilled print workers, to become the Graphical, Paper and Media Union (GPMU) and in 2004, the GPMU became part of Amicus.

Fleet Street has enjoyed the diversity of over a dozen national daily and Sunday newspapers with differing political stances. Whilst powerful newspaper proprietors such as Northcliffe, Beaverbrook, Maxwell and Murdoch greatly influenced the content of their papers, there were also many famous editors and a raft of journalists, including foreign and war correspondents, experienced writers, political reporters, 'firemen' who were dispatched to report from crisis venues, and crime, sports, showbiz and gossip writers. Many achieved legendary status through their writing or their exploits, or both. Columnists in the post war period helped to shape the views of both the papers and the public.

Many lamented the departure of the press from Fleet Street. The late Keith Waterhouse wrote:

O farewell then, the Street of Ink, aka the Street of Adventure, aka the Street of Shame, aka the Boulevard of Broken Dreams, aka Fleet Street . . . When I first came down to Fleet

Street in the middle of the last century it reeked of printer's ink and fair throbbed with life. With its mighty presses rumbling and roaring it sounded like a small industrial town, which indeed was what it was.

Similarly William Deedes, editor of the *Daily Telegraph*, 1974-1986, said,

> When I arrived in Fleet Street in 1931, almost every upstairs window had a provincial newspaper office behind it. What was extraordinary is that in this, the main road through central London, there were these giant factories. There were always lorries arriving by day loaded with newsprint, vans flying out at night to take the editions to the railway stations. The newspapers had printing presses thundering below street level. Then there were the pubs which were where we used to drink more than we should. In a sense we were much more comrades and colleagues than today

The beginning of the end of Fleet Street's association with the press came in the 1980s. The industry had industrial-relations problems in the 1970s, particularly when the *Times*, because of a strike, did not appear for nearly a year. In 1985, Robert Maxwell had secured a twenty-five per cent reduction in manning at the *Mirror*, and changes in technology saw inevitable replacements in most traditional printing jobs. In 1986 Rupert Murdoch moved the production of his papers – *The Times, Sunday Times, News of the World, Sun*, to a non-union plant at Wapping. The days of the composing room along with NGA union cards and a rulebook are no doubt fondly remembered. It was not long after Murdoch's exodus that other newspapers embraced the changes and vacated Fleet Street to locations in east London. Veteran journalist, Roy Greenslade, former editor of the *Daily Mirror* described Fleet Street as the 'Street of Shame'. He added that it was:

> Absolutely wonderful, a 24-hour village permanently en fete. Boozed-up journalists were all over the place. When I was on the *Sunday Mirror*, one reporter's regular habit was to return from lunch and his head would gradually sink into his typewriter. It was fine. I was sorry when the Press Association went, I was sorry when Reuters went. It's always sad to see another bit vanish from Fleet Street.

One outpost remains (at the time of writing) at No. 185, where a dozen editorial staff from the *Dundee Courier*, the *Sunday Post* and the *Weekly News* – part of the DC Thomson publishing group – report from London on behalf of their readers in Scotland.

CHAPTER SEVEN

LITERATURE ABOUT FLEET STREET

Building on the presence and literary culture of booksellers, printers, newspapers, and various types of publications, Fleet Street has also been the inspiration for writers, and has provided the setting for many novels. These include *A Vicious Circle* (1996) by Amanda Craig, which satirizes, in part, the world of publishing, and *My Name Is Legion* (2004) by A. N. Wilson. Wilson's book is set in the first years of the twenty-first century and revolves around two main topics – the gutter press and Christian religion.

A Crooked Sixpence by Murray Sayle was published in 1961, but was pulped shortly after because of libel threats from a near-penniless London aristocrat who believed that he was identifiable in the story. Forty-seven years later it was republished. It tells the story of a young Australian reporter, brimming with enthusiasm and ambition, and his subsequent disillusionment. He arrives to work for a mass-circulation Fleet Street Sunday scandal sheet. Sayle himself moved to London in 1952 and worked in Fleet Street – mainly as a daily casual reporter for *The People* – until 1956. *A Crooked Sixpence* has been described as the most keenly observed book on Fleet Street manners and mores that has ever been written.

Two of the best 'Fleet Street novels' are *Towards the End of the Morning* (1967) by Michael Frayn and *Scoop* (1938) by Evelyn Waugh. Frayn's book is satirical, and is about journalists working on a British newspaper during the heyday of Fleet Street. The protagonists work to compile the miscellaneous parts of the newspaper such as the 'nature notes' column, the religious 'thought for the day', and the crossword. The journalists' work is extremely dull. At the heart of the story are two journalists – the older and ambitious John Dyson, who is anxious to find an easy route out of his mundane job, and the younger, more laid back Bob Bell. The two of them work in the crossword and nature notes department, but spend most of their time in the local drinking establishments, complaining about their jobs and their workloads whilst the paper appears to be in a state of torpor.

> Various members of the staff emerged from Hand and Ball Passage during the last dark hour of the morning, walked with an air of sober responsibility towards the main entrance, greeted the commissionaire and vanished upstairs in the lift to telephone their friends and draw their expenses before going out again to have lunch.

Jay was the last frequenter of the Cheshire Cheese who knew the men who had known Johnson.

An unsavoury incident was reported by the *Morning Herald and Daily Advertiser* of 9 August 1784, about an attempted murder at the Cheese. A porter in the Temple named John Gromont persuaded a woman who had deserted him, to accept a drink at the Cheshire Cheese, and then 'in a fit of frenzy he cut the woman's throat'.

However, the Cheese was better known for its hearty meals and puddings. A brochure entitled *Round London* (1725), described the tavern, as an 'eating house for goodly fare'. The *Reporter*, on 28 October 1874, wrote:

> We have occasionally used this old-fashioned house for over a quarter of a century, and can conscientiously assert that for its chops and steaks, cold beef and salad, and marvellous rump-steak pudding, and for the alacrity with which these edibles are supplied the establishment is unmatchable in the metropolis.

The Evening Standard of 10 January 1867 commented: 'The Cheshire Cheese is famous for steak-pudding, agreeably tempered by kidneys, larks, and oysters.'

Its fame was reported in the United States. Miss Sarah Morton, a special correspondent of the *Illustrated Buffalo Express* of New York, 15 February 1891, gave an account of this English specialty:

> It was the night of the beef-steak pudding, a delicacy served only twice a week, and in precisely the same way that it has been served in this very place for 200 years . . . There is my big dinner plate piled high with what on earth! Birds! yes, tiny bits of birds, skylarks, kidneys, strips of beef, just smothered in pastry like sea-foam, and dark brown gravy, steaming with fragrance, as seasoning . . . Then came stewed cheese, on the thin shaving of crisp, golden toast in hot silver saucers so hot that the cheese was of the substance of thick cream, the flavour of purple pansies and red raspberries commingled.

Visitors today will find two ground floor rooms. One is a dark paneled bar with a portrait of William Simpson, who started as a waiter in 1829, which was to be passed down to future landlords. The Chop Room has high backed settles that have been arranged back-to-back to create small booths. A portrait of Dr. Johnson hangs on a wall, and another painting of Johnson and his biographer, James Boswell, was found in a cellar relatively recently and has been restored. The narrow and awkward steps that lead down to the cellar bars reveal the discovery of the vaults, a fascinating series of small, stone rooms. The steps continue into the cellar proper, where a further bar and dining area can be found.

West of the Cheshire Cheese is another old historic pub, Ye Olde Cock Tavern, which originally stood opposite the present pub. Like the Cheshire Cheese, the Cock survived the Great Fire and can be traced back to the sixteenth century. It was once called the Cock and Bottle as the *Intelligencer* of 1665 noted in an advertisement regarding the impact of the Great Fire: 'This is to notify that the master of the Cock and Bottle, commonly called the Cock Alehouse at Temple Bar, hath dismissed his servants and shut up his house, for this Long Vacation; intending (God willing) to return at Michaelmas next.' Samuel Pepys knew the Cock well. In one of his many flirtations he brought the attractive actress Mrs. Knipp to the tavern: 'Thence by water to the Temple, and thence to the Cock Alehouse, and drank and did eat a lobster, and sang, and mighty merry.' It was particularly famous for its chops, steaks and porter.

The old gilt cock over the portal is believed to have been carved by Grinling Gibbons (1648-1721), and the old tavern had many famous literary associations. It has been frequented by Ben Jonson, Pepys and Alfred, Lord Tennyson (1809-1892). Tennyson's poem *Will Waterproof's Lyrical Monologue* was written at the Cock in 1842 and included the following lines:

O plump head-waiter at The Cock,
To which I most resort,
How goes the time? 'Tis five o'clock.
Go fetch a pint of port:
But let it not be such as that
You set before chance-comers,
But such whose father-grape grew fat
On Lusitanian summers . . .

Head-waiter, honour'd by the guest
Half-mused, or reeling-ripe,
The pint, you brought me, was the best
That ever came from pipe.
But tho' the port surpasses praise,
My nerves have dealt with stiffer.
Is there some magic in the place?
Or do my peptics differ?

In the twentieth century, Virginia Woolf dined in the evenings at the Cock and T.S. Eliot also frequented the pub.

In 1887, the reason why the Cock literally crossed the road was to make way for the Law Courts branch of the Bank of England. Much of the Cock's interior was carefully installed in the new building, including the fireplace and the ornamental cockerel. It is the narrowest building on Fleet Street. Tragically, in 1990 a fire broke out and destroyed many of the original ornaments.

Freemasonry has its origins in the alehouse, notably the Goose and Gridiron, which was located in St. Paul's Churchyard. On 24 June 1717, four craft Lodges met there and constituted themselves as a Grand Lodge. Not surprisingly, the most overt Masonic presence was in the City of London. Nonetheless there was a preponderance of taverns and inns along Fleet Street in which Freemasons met. For example it was reported that the: 'Grand Lodge met at the Devil, Temple Bar 20 May 1725 with former Grand Officers . . .' Rival lodges began to meet at the Mitre Tavern in Fleet Street in 1768, and continued meeting there until 1781 when they moved to Freemason's Hall in Great Queen Street. Other Masonic lodges on Fleet Street included Crown, St. Dunstan's; Globe Tavern; Jacob's Ladder, Bolt and Tun; Caledonian Lodge Globe; Manchester Lodge, at the Maidenhead, Ram Court; Horn Tavern and the Cheshire Cheese.

At the eastern end of Fleet Street are the Tipperary and the Punch Tavern. The Tipperary was built on the edge of a monastery. The original name, The Boars Head, survived until just after the First World War, when the Irish print workers returning from the trenches

*The Cock of the Olde Cock Tavern on
Fleet Street*

*The original Irish pub outside of
Ireland*

The Punch Tavern sign

renamed it after the popular song, *It's a Long Way to Tipperary* (1912). The Irish origin of the pub goes back to around the year 1700, when S. G. Mooney and Son brewery chain of Dublin bought the pub. It now proudly proclaims itself as 'London's Original Irish Pub'. It also makes the equally bold claim to be the first pub in the whole world outside Ireland to serve Guinness. The present building dates back to 1605 and managed to survive the Great Fire largely intact, thanks to its stone and brick construction. It was fitted in traditional Irish style, with a clock made by the famous clockmaker Thomas Campion (1638-1713), but this was later stolen. In the 1960s Greene King bought the Tipperary, and later refurbished it in the style of Mooney's days.

Saville and Martin built the present Punch Tavern in 1894-5 on the site of a previous building known as the Crown and Sugar Loaf, the name of the nearby pub in St. Bride's Lane. The Punch Tavern was renamed because of its association with the satirical magazine *Punch*, which was conceived in a pub near here in 1841, and whose journalists frequented it. This connection was celebrated when the pub used to display many of the magazine's cartoons on its walls. The pub is a Grade II listed building with many original Victorian features including a glazed, tiled entrance hall with etched glass doors, mirrors, barrel-vaulted ceiling, ten six-foot mirrors, marble bar, dark oak panelling, ornate fireplace, and a series of original Punch and Judy themed paintings.

Other present day drinking places on and around Fleet Street include the impressive Grade 1 listed Bank of England, which was built in 1888, in the Italianate style, as a branch of the Bank of England to serve the nearby Law Courts. Fuller's renovated the building in the 1990s. The Slug and Lettuce on Fetter Lane; Serjeants, Old Mitre Court – the little square contains some characteristic Georgian houses; Witness Box, Tudor Street, which lawyers and journalists frequented; Coach and Horses, Whitefriars Street; Harrow, a Grade II listed pub built in 1826 that was once a legendary Fleet Street

The ornate ceiling in the Punch

The Old Bell on Fleet Street

drinking haunt when the *Sun* was based opposite; The Old Bell, Fleet Street, built in the 1670s it has a long association with Fleet Street's printers, and St. Bride's Tavern, Bridewell Place.

El Vino's is a Fleet Street institution. Known as Bower and Co. it was founded in 1879 by Alfred Louis Bower, who started as a wine merchant on Mark Lane, on the eastern side of the City of London. Bower's business did well with the increasing demand for the Bordeaux, Burgundy, and Sherry that he imported. With this success, a further four wine bars in the City and West End opened. In 1915, Alfred Bower set out to achieve his ambition of becoming Lord Mayor, when he stood as an Alderman. However, the problem was, that in order to stand, he would have to cease trading in the City under his own name. Consequently, the company name was changed in 1923 to El Vino, and Bower became Lord Mayor between 1924 and 1925.

His nephew, a flamboyant character, Francis (Frank) Bower succeeded him, and it was he who developed the 'house rule' of never selling a wine he did not consider ready to drink himself. El Vino's was very popular with journalists. Writer and journalist G.K. Chesterton (1874-1936) drank prodigiously here. El Vino's had a strict policy about serving women at the bar, and had a dress code that required a jacket and tie. Chris Moncrieff of the Press Association said that

> El Vino's was once a sacred male haunt in Fleet Street, to which women were admitted only with a male escort. Women were not allowed to stand at the bar or buy drinks. Some 20 years ago the daunting ladies of Fleet Street invaded the place and demanded equality. It was a daunting spectacle and terrified the management and most of the customers.

Although not a tavern, a well known drinking and eating establishment on Fleet Street was Dick's Coffee House, which was kept for some time during the reign of George II (1727-1760) by a Mrs. Yarrow and her daughter. The poet William Cowper (1731-1800) showed the first symptoms of derangement when he read a letter in a newspaper at Dick's, which he believed had been written to drive him to suicide. He went away and tried to hang himself. In a piece of tragic comedy, his suicide failed because the garter he used broke.

Another well-known establishment was the Rainbow Tavern, which started life as a coffee house. It was the second to be established in London, and was opened by James Farr in 1657. Shortly after it was opened, Farr found himself in trouble, and was presented for making and selling:

> [A drink] called coffee, whereby, in making the same, he annoyeth his neighbours by the evil smells, and for keeping of fire the most part night and day, whereby his chimney and chamber has been set on fire, to the great danger of his neighbours.

By the late nineteenth century the Rainbow Tavern became the meeting place for the Rainbow Circle, a political group consisting of Liberals, Fabians and socialists, who first met there 1894. It included such luminaries as Ramsay MacDonald, Charles Trevelyan and Sydney Olivier. The circle had its own journal, *Progressive Review*, which in its first issue in 1896 expressed dismay at the decline of the Liberal Party. However, in 1896 they moved the venue for their gatherings to a member's house in Bloomsbury Square, a decision prompted by a dispute in the tavern over a dinner of 'boiled cod so poor and

El Vino's, a Fleet Street institution

watery that even philosophers turned against it'. The Circle survived until 1966 when they disbanded. The Rainbow features in the short story *The Misplaced Attachment Of Mr. John Dounce* (1836) by Charles Dickens where he comments:

> There was once a fine collection of old boys to be seen round the circular table at Offley's every night, between the hours of half-past eight and half-past eleven. We have lost sight of them for some time. There were, and may be still, for aught we know, two splendid specimens in full blossom at the Rainbow Tavern in Fleet Street, who always used to sit in the box nearest the fireplace, and smoked long cherry-stick pipes which went under the table, with the bowls resting on the floor. Grand old boys they were – fat, red-faced, white-headed old fellows – always there – one on one side the table, and the other opposite – puffing and drinking away in great state. Everybody knew them, and it was supposed by some people that they were both immortal.

A pub that closed down in recent times is the King and Keys, which stood next door to the Mary Queen of Scots building, near the Cheshire Cheese. Evidence of it can still be seen, with its green exterior and the name between the windows. With its authentic flagstone floors and chest of drawers behind the bar, the pub was once the haunt of *Daily Telegraph* journalists. Peregrine Worsthorne, editor of the *Sunday Telegraph* between 1986 and 1989, commented that alcohol was a problem. 'The Telegraph pub was the King and Keys – the scene of drunken misbehaviour, rows and boxing matches

. . . Pandemonium! Fleet Street was a gathering of eccentrics . . . It was Grub Street, Gin Alley.'

As early as 1885, Henry Vigar-Harris in his book *London at Midnight* commented that some of the public houses in Fleet Street

> are only closed for two out of the 24 hours, and the men who occupy their sawdusted parlours are the outcasts of the literary world. Some of these men have been in prominent positions on our leading daily press, and held high appointments on the staff of provincial papers, but in consequence of their debauched habits they have been dethroned.

Roy Greenslade, a media commentator for many years, notably for the *Guardian* reflected:

> It's true that pubs did play an inordinate role in Fleet Street life. The names spring easily to mind . . . and others known exclusively by their nicknames, such as the Stab in the Back [White Hart], Aunties and the Mucky Duck [White Swan]. Many journalists drank through the day and on into the early hours at the Press Club. Daily life was punctuated by drink. Liquid lunches were common.

The relationship between those in the newspaper industry and the drinking holes of Fleet Street was unique, and became the stuff of legend. Canary Wharf could never create such a culture.

Opposite: *The name of the old King and Keys can still be made out between the windows*

CHAPTER TEN

(OTHER) FAMOUS RESIDENTS

Many famous people of Fleet Street have already been discussed. Given the importance of the street as a principal thoroughfare connecting the City and the West End, it is inevitable that many pageants and processions of the great and the good have passed through. These have included Lord Mayor's Shows, Queen Victoria's Jubilees and the entry of monarchs as well as notable funerals such as those of Nelson in 1805 and Wellington in 1852.

Notable residents of the street date back to at least the fourteenth century. For example, in the fifteenth century, the Pastons, whose family letters between 1422 and 1509 give us such a vivid picture of life in the Middle Ages, lived there. Sir John Paston had his town house in Fleet Street, and among the Letters are several references to the street. By the sixteenth century Fleet Street became the centre, not only of literary activity, but also of fashion. Sir Amias Paulet (1532-1588) gaoler to Mary Queen of Scots until her execution in 1587 wrote to the Secretary of State, Sir Francis Walsingham from 'my poor lodging in Fleet Street', in 1588.

Shakespeare's connection with Fleet Street is, to say the least, a tenuous one, but references in his plays form a link between him and Clement's Inn, York House, the Temple Gardens, and Middle Temple where *Twelfth Night* was performed in 1601. The best we can speculate is that it is thought that he probably directed the performance, or at least was present during its progress. His contemporary, Ben Jonson, lived at Temple Bar at a comb maker's shop, which stood on the south side of the street.

The great English poet John Milton (1608-1674) lodged, in 1639, with a tailor at a house in St. Bride's Churchyard. It was not a happy episode in Milton's life. When his first wife, Mary Powell, lived there she found it very solitary and left at the outbreak of Civil War to live with her Royalist parents. Desertion prompted Milton over the next few years to publish a series of pamphlets including his famous *Doctrine and Discipline of Divorce* (1643).

Izaak Walton (1593-1683), author of *The Complete Angler* (1653) lived in Fleet Street. In 1614 he had a linen draper's shop two doors west of Chancery Lane and became friendly with the poet John Donne, then vicar of St. Dunstan's between 1624 and 1631. Poet Abraham Cowley (1618-1667) was born in 1618 in a house that adjoined Serjeants' Inn.

Between 1673 and 1682 John Dryden (1631-1700), one of the most influential literary figures of the late seventeenth century, lived close to Salisbury Court.

A figure better known for his name than any particular achievements was Praise-God Barebone, after whom the Barebones Parliament of 1653 was named. His parents, who were zealous Puritans, named him Unless-Jesus-Christ-Had-Died-For-Thee-Thou-Hadst-Been-Damned Barebone (1598-1679). He was a leather seller as well as a preacher and a Fifth Monarchist (believers in the imminent second coming of Christ). His house was by the sign of the *Lock and Key*. Another Civil War association is with General George Monk who was responsible for leading the parliamentary troops into London from Scotland in 1660, and thus opening the way for the Restoration of monarchy under King Charles II. In 1659 Monk wrote a letter to Lady Rachel Vaughan asking that his old lodging be taken up for him in Fleet Street near the Conduit. Many references to Fleet Street are made in the diaries of Samuel Pepys and John Evelyn, especially visits to various taverns.

The eighteenth century produced many illustrious people who once graced Fleet Street. Literary figures such as Swift, Steele, and Addison among others have already been mentioned, and Samuel Johnson's presence is so pervasive, especially around the inns and coffee houses. In 1748 Johnson came to 17 Gough Square where, after years of toil and dogged persistence and the help of six amanuenses, he compiled his great Dictionary in 1755. Over two and a half centuries later the Liberal Member of Parliament, Cecil Harmsworth, purchased Johnson's house in 1911. By this time it was derelict and run down. Harmsworth restored the House to its original condition and opened it to the public in 1912. During the Second World War Johnson's House was nearly destroyed on three occasions during bombing raids. Fortunately it was saved by the Auxiliary Fire Service who were conveniently using the House as a rest centre. Today the House is run by the Dr Johnson's House Trust and is open to the public.

Across the square, facing the house is a statue of Hodge (unveiled in 1997), Dr. Johnson's favourite cat immortalised in a passage in James Bowell's *Life of Johnson*: 'I never shall forget the indulgence with which he treated Hodge, his cat: for whom he himself used to go out and buy oysters, lest the servants having that trouble should take a dislike to the poor creature.' The statue shows Hodge sitting on Johnson's famous dictionary with the inscription 'a very fine cat indeed'.

Writer and poet Oliver Goldsmith (1730-1774) wrote his best-known work *The Vicar of Wakefield*, when he lived in Wine Office Court. Goldsmith was a familiar figure around the Fleet Street area and ended his days in Brick Court just off Middle Temple Lane. Near Temple Church is a plain stone inscribed with the words, 'Here Lies Oliver Goldsmith'. It would be more accurate to say that this is the approximate spot where his remains are buried.

A more tragic figure was the poet Thomas Chatterton (1752-1770), who committed suicide at the young age of seventeen. He moved to London from Bristol hoping to make a living as a poet. Chatterton is famous for fabricating the poetry of a 15th century Bristol monk called Thomas Rowley. Chatterton certainly influenced the Romantics such as Keats, Wordsworth and Coleridge. On August 24 1770 he committed suicide by arsenic poisoning and was buried in the Shoe Lane Workhouse Cemetery. The site no longer exists and the whereabouts of his remains is not known.

At the corner of Fleet Street and Whitefriars Street lived the famous clockmaker Thomas Tompion (1639–1713), known as the father of English watchmaking. His work

Plaque to Dr Johnson outside his house

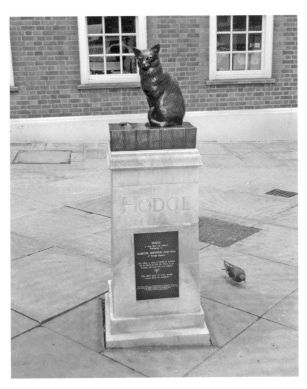

Left: *Statue of Hodge, Dr. Johnson's favourite cat in Gough Square*
Right: *Oliver Goldsmith's house in Wine Office Court, drawn by Hanslip Fletcher*

A plaque to the great
watchmakers, William Tompion
and George Graham

includes some of the most important clocks and watches in the world, and he was one of the few watchmakers to become a member of the Royal Society. When the Royal Observatory was established in 1676, King Charles II selected Tompion to create two clocks based on an escapement designed by Richard Towneley that would be wound only once a year. He also made some of the first watches with balance springs. These were much more accurate than earlier watches. In 1711 Tompion joined in partnership with his apprentice George Graham (1674-1751), who also lived at the same address. Graham, like Tompion, was a Quaker and was buried in the same tomb as his friend and mentor Tompion in Westminster Abbey. A plaque in Fleet Street commemorates both of them.

East of St. Dunstan's Church, next to Fetter Lane, is Crane Court, first mentioned in 1662. The Court was destroyed in the Great Fire, and rebuilt. At the beginning of the eighteenth century Dr. Edward Browne, President of the (Royal) College of Physicians, lived here and held meetings at his house. The Philosophical Society later used the house and the poet Samuel Taylor Coleridge (1772-1834) delivered twelve lectures on Shakespeare there in 1819. The house was burned down in 1877.

The great essayist William Hazlitt (1778-1830) lived on the first floor of No. 3 Bouverie Street in 1829, the year before he died. One of his most famous books is *Political Essays with Sketches of Public Characters* (1819) in which he explains how the admiration of power turns many writers into 'intellectual pimps and hirelings of the press', an apt statement in the context of Fleet Street.

Statue of Kaled a character from Byron's poem, Lara

From very small beginnings was how Louis Rothman (1869-1926) began. Rothman, who was founder of Rothmans International, one of the United Kingdom's largest tobacco companies, built his business in Fleet Street. He came to England in 1887 from the Ukraine and in 1890 opened his own business, a small kiosk at 55a, Fleet Street, where he sold cigarettes that he had rolled the night before for the reporters and printers of the area. This allowed him to open two more shops. In 1900 he opened a showroom in Pall Mall, and from there he traded as *Rothmans of Pall Mall* to distinguish his business from that of his brother Max who traded from Regent Street.

Plaques or statues often commemorate notable individuals and a number of these can be found in various places on and around Fleet Street. Some have already been mentioned. No.1 Fleet Street displays a plaque denoting the site of the Devil Tavern. Opposite on the corner of Chancery Lane is the statue of Kaled, sculptured in white stone. This was placed in the alcove of the pawnbrokers and jewellery emporium of Messrs George Attenborough & Co in the 1870s, when the building was first erected. Kaled is a character from Byron's narrative poem, *Lara*: 'The colour of young Kaled went and came, the lip of ashes, and the cheek of flame.'

Plaque to the Automobile Association office which opened in 1905

Along Chancery Lane is a plaque that reads, *Site of Old Serjeants' Inn, 1415-1910*. At No. 18 Fleet Street, the Automobile Association opened its first office in this building in 1905. A plaque erected in 1965 was unveiled to mark the Diamond Jubilee of the AA.

Along Middle Temple Lane can be found a plaque to the antiquary and astrologer Elias Ashmole (1617-1692) who once lived there. The Ashmolean Museum in Oxford, completed in 1683, contains much of his collection and is considered to be the first truly public museum in Europe. Other associations with Middle Temple Lane are poet William Cowper, who lived there in 1752; writer Charles Lamb resided between 1809 and 1817; and Dr. Johnson lived at No.1 for five years (1760-1765). In 1804 an opticians shop in the Lane sold the first barometers ever seen in London.

Also on Middle Temple Lane is a plaque which reads:

> This building is named the Carpmael Building in recognition of the signal services rendered to the Middle Temple by Master Kenneth Carpmael QC in connection with the restoration of the Inn after the war of 1939-1945.

In the area of Temple Church, formerly the cloister courtyard of the monastery of the Knights Templar, is a memorial to Sir John Gurney which translates:

To John Gurney, bearer of Arms, Treasurer, He restored and conserved the south part, which is his own, of the Inn of the Inner Temple. 1827.

In the centre of Church Court facing Temple Church is a ten-metre-high column which has a bronze image of a horse mounted by two riders. It is derived from the seal of the knights, who were originally too poor to have a horse each. The same image can be seen in the east window of the church. The column also marks the point at which the Great Fire of 1666 was extinguished.

Also within Inner Temple is the Littleton Building, which stands on the site of the former Niblett Hall. The original building, Niblett Hall, was erected in 1932 out of a legacy from William Charles Niblett of Singapore, barrister of the Inn. It was demolished in 1992 to make way for the Littleton Building. The Pegasus from the Niblett building survives and adorns the entrance. Close by, an information board states that the column in this court was erected and dedicated in the year 2000 AD, in the centre of what was formerly the cloister courtyard of the monastery of the Knights Templar.

In the south west corner of Crown Office Row is the present day Lamb Building, built in 1954 as part of a reconstruction following bombing during the Second World War. The first building to be constructed on this site was converted into chambers in the late 16th century, and was then pulled down and rebuilt in 1639 with the new building called Elm Court Building. The original Lamb Building was located in Lamb Court south east of Temple Church. This building stood on the original burial ground of the Knights Templar, and had been rebuilt after the Great Fire of 1666. A ground plaque shows the original position of this building, and there is also an information board at 2 Crown Office Row that marks the birthplace of writer Charles Lamb (1775-1834) who once said 'The man must have a rare recipe for melancholy, who can be dull in Fleet Street.'

Still in the area of Inner Temple is Fig Tree Court, Inner Temple. An oval plaque on the wall states: 'Fig Tree Court adjoined this ancient buttery, 1515-1666. It was destroyed in the Great Fire of London, rebuilt in 1679 and again destroyed by enemy action 1940'. Nearby, an information board reads: 'The end of Inner Temple Hall facing Elm Court is the Knights' medieval crypt and buttery, the oldest rooms still in use in the Temple'.

Moving east towards Old Mitre Court is the Francis Taylor building, erected in 1957 and named after Sir Francis Kyffin Taylor (1854-1951), who held many prestigious legal offices. In 1918, he was invested as a Knight Commander, Order of the British Empire (K.B.E.) and later as a Knight Grand Cross, Order of the British Empire (G.B.E.) in 1929. For his services to the judiciary he was created 1st Baron Maenan, of Ellesmere on 29 June 1948. He lived to the grand age of ninety-eight and died only three years after he retired from the bench, making him one of the oldest serving judges in Great Britain. A plaque on the wall is dedicated to his memory.

Along Fleet Street on the south side is Bouverie Street, where a Corporation of the City of London plaque notes that the great literary critic and essayist William Hazlitt (1778-1830) lived in a house on this site in 1829. Hazlitt was stricken in health, and living in some degree of poverty by the time he occupied the first floor of No. 3 Bouverie Street. The following year he died at Frith Street, Soho. Further south along Bouverie Street is Magpie Alley, which leads to the Whitefriars crypt. One entire wall of Magpie Alley is covered in tiles telling the story of printing.

Back onto Fleet Street, directly on the north side at St Dunstan-in-the-West Church, are a number of interesting memorials. The statue of Queen Elizabeth I, which was

Drinking Fountain, 1868 outside St. Dunstan's Church

discussed earlier, stands on the east side of the entrance to the church. A bust of Lord Northcliffe, unveiled in 1930, stands in front of the church, whilst a water fountain is situated outside the entrance. Around the bowl it reads: 'The fear of the Lord is a fountain of life'. It was erected in 1860 and is a good example of surviving Victorian street furniture. On the east-facing wall to the left of the Northcliffe bust is a plaque to J. L. Garvin (1868-1947), who was editor of the *Observer* for thirty-four years. Also next to St. Dunstan's on the east side is the London offices of D. C. Thomson, which they have owned for something like 100 years. The titles of famous Scottish newspapers and magazines adorn the sides of the building.

Moving east we come to Red Lion Court, and although there is no plaque here, there is an interesting sign. The court, which was named after the Red Lion Tavern, destroyed in the Great Fire, was once a place of publishing, and where the *Gentleman's Magazine* was published from 1781. The court now comprises mainly of offices, but there is a K2 telephone box and a printer's sign, which belonged to Abraham Valpy (1787–1854). The sign on the wall depicts a hand pouring oil into a Greek lamp and dates from the 1820s. It has a motto that reads, '*Alere Flammam*' (feed the flame). Valpy came to Red Lion Court in 1822 and published editions of classical writers until around 1837 when he retired, leaving just his mark on the wall.

*Sign of the Abraham Valpy, once a
printer in Red Lion Court*

Next to Red Lion Court is Johnson's Court, which leads into Gough Square (more like an L shaped court than a square) where Dr. Johnson lived. His house, now the Johnson Museum, is open to the public. Facing the house there is a statue of his cat Hodge that was erected in 1997. The cat is seated on *A Dictionary of the English Language* and has oyster shells at his paws, a luxury in which Johnson indulged him. The Goughs owned Gough Square, a family of wool merchants in the eighteenth century. Adjoining Gough Square is Gunpowder Square, complete with a cannon, which was placed there in 1989.

Walking from Gough Square back to Fleet Street there are a number of interesting places in close proximity. The Tipperary pub on the south side was built on the site of a monastery and has the River Fleet running beneath it. A plaque outside gives the history of the pub. Next door to the Tipperary is a plaque to the clockmakers Tompion and Graham. Across the road is the famous Cheshire Cheese pub where, in Wine Office Court, an information board reads:

> Sir said Dr Johnson if you wish to have a just notion of the magnitude of this great City you must not be satisfied with seeing its great streets and squares but must survey the innumerable little lames and courts.

Above: *Plaque to T. P. O'Connor*

Opposite: *Mary Queen of Scots Building next door to the Cheshire Cheese*

Next door to the Cheshire Cheese is Mary Queen of Scots House built in 1905. There is a statue of Mary overlooking the shop below. The connection with Mary Queen of Scots stems from a romantic idea of the developer Sir John Tollemache MP, who was a great admirer of Mary.

Heading east on the south side is a bust of the journalist and parliamentarian, T. P. O'Connor (1848-1929), erected in 1936. O'Connor founded and was the first editor of several newspapers and journals including the *Star* (1887) and *Weekly Sun* (1891). He was appointed the first President of the Board of Film Censors in 1917, and was appointed to the Privy Council by the first Labour government in 1924.

To the side of O'Connor's bust is Salisbury Court, which derives its name from the great house and gardens of the Bishop of Salisbury from the mid-thirteenth century. Centuries later it came into the possession of the Earls of Dorset, and was known as Dorset Square and Dorset Court for a time. There are two plaques along Salisbury Street. One is to Samuel Pepys, who was born here, and the other notes that Henry White published the first copy of the *Sunday Times* on 20 October 1822.

Further south along Salisbury Court is a plaque and obelisk to the Mayoralty, which was officially dedicated in 1990. Opposite in Dorset Rise is a nine-metre-high statue of St George and the Dragon by Michael Sandle, erected in 1988. On Dorset Road is a plaque denoting the site of the Salisbury Court Playhouse, 1629-1649. Further south on John Carpenter Street is a complex of buildings built to house the Guildhall School of Music. Each of the five oculi on the first floor are decorated and surmounted with a name carved in stone which read, left to right: Tallis, Gibbons, Purcell, Arne, Sterndale-Bennett.

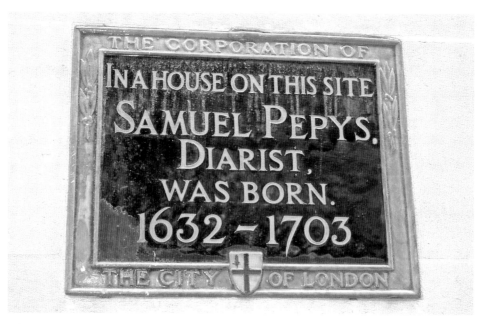

Above: *Plaque to Samuel Pepys*

Opposite: *St George and the Dragon by Michael Sandle, 1988 in Dorset Rise*

The list of famous journalists who worked in Fleet Street is inevitably a long one. Among those commemorated with plaques are crime writer Edgar Wallace (1875-1832). Wallace, at age eleven, sold newspapers at Ludgate Circus, where a plaque commemorates him. After many jobs he became a war correspondent for the *Daily Mail* in South Africa during the Boer War, but was sacked for writing a libellous article. He turned to writing crime thrillers and is credited with inventing the modern thriller novel. Wallace was very prolific, writing more than 170 books, which at one time were selling at a rate of five million books a year. Although he earned a fortune, he lost it all as a result of his extravagant lifestyle. West of Temple Bar in Essex Street, the Edgar Wallace pub can be found.

Fleet Street has many historic associations. Although it will always be linked with the press, despite the exodus of national papers from the mid 1980s, there are so many other fascinating stories to tell. The famous River Fleet, religious houses, legal quarters, pubs, printing houses, the many colourful characters and events have all left a rich legacy. Fleet Street can claim even those seemingly trivial, but essential, features of life. The first modern public lavatory was erected at 95 Fleet Street in 1852. It was for men only and was discreetly called a 'public waiting room.' Another, possibly contentious, claim is the first pillar-box, erected in 1855 at the corner of Farringdon Street and Fleet Street. Before this date, people had taken their letters to receiving offices, or relied on itinerant collectors. There were ten collections a day, between the hours of 9am and 10pm. Fleet Street may no longer have the atmosphere or vibrancy it once had, but there is still much to discover along this street and its many fascinating tributaries.